S0-CNB-993

THE GOD BOX

THE GOD BOX

Hope Strength Courage @ Your Fingertips

For Steve Avella

With gratitude.

Lynn Neu
Nov. 2, 2022

LYNN NEU

Copyright © 2009 by Lynn C. Neu.

Library of Congress Control Number:		2009906844
ISBN:	Hardcover	978-1-4415-5390-4
	Softcover	978-1-4415-5389-8

All rights reserved. No part of this book may be reproduced or transmitted in any form or by any means, electronic or mechanical, including photocopying, recording, or by any information storage and retrieval system, without permission in writing from the copyright owner.

This book was printed in the United States of America.

To order additional copies of this book, contact:
Xlibris Corporation
1-888-795-4274
www.Xlibris.com
Orders@Xlibris.com
57924

For Julie

All will be well

Contents

Foreword

It was a hot July day in 1976, and we were starting a new summer session at Loyola University of Chicago's Institute of Pastoral Studies. I looked forward to meeting the new students and getting the course underway. A young woman, who had just driven in the extreme heat from Racine, arrived just in time for class. By looking at her, you would never have guessed that she was "one of them." How could you guess that? She was wearing a yellow tank top and white shorts! Quite fetching as I recall.

I had asked my mentor, Fr. Leo Mahon, one of the most successful pastors in Chicago, how he did it. How come every parish he took over came alive and really flourished? He let me in on his secret. "When I go to a new parish, I seek out those women and men in the parish who, at one time in their lives, entertained the notion of a vocation to religious life or priesthood. They may have decided such a life was not for them, but at one time, they seriously entertained 'the call.' That never goes away. It remains part of them. So all I do is 'call them' to service in the parish. More often than not, they respond enthusiastically." At the time of our first meeting, I had no way of knowing that the fetching Lynn Neu was "one of them," an especially gifted "one of them." What did become immediately clear was that Lynn was a high-energy person who had a special gift of relating to people, just the sort of person particularly well suited to ministry. It was no surprise to anyone who knew her that she ultimately discerned that the "call" she was experiencing was not to the life of a Dominican nun but to a life of Christian ministry *within the Catholic Church*. Not an easy thing for a woman back then, nor now, for that matter.

That Lynn Neu is a real ministerial treasure is evidenced by the fact that she has held only three different ministry jobs in her lifetime. As she herself says in chapter 10, "I've only held three career-related jobs in my lifetime, all in ministry, each a ten—to seventeen-year stint, each requiring leadership skills—teaching, directing, facilitating, etc." She has worked at all levels of ministry open to women and has even served in positions never before held by a woman, e.g., her work at the Archdiocesan level in Milwaukee. If you're a woman, and if they keep you at those sorts of jobs for a decade or more, that is concrete recognition of your abilities and gifts.

Lynn has always attracted people; she's always been a pied piper, people-magnet sort of person. But be careful; when you get close, she'll ask you to do something. Lynn never works alone; her ministry always becomes a "group ministry." Listen to her describe this aspect of her life.

> My ability to ask was strengthened on a student retreat where we "picked a promise" to live by for the year. I chose "seek and you will find; knock and the door will be opened to you" (Mt 7). We were instructed to simplify the passage, put it in our own words so we'd remember it easily, and then decorate a candle with our simple words. The words on my candle? "Just ask!"

> I love to put people to work doing good things. It boosts their confidence, and good things get done! And I've noticed, people rather like being asked. I think it has something to do with trust. It wouldn't be easy to ask people to do things if I didn't trust that the need was worthy, or didn't trust them to recognize the importance of the need, or didn't trust they could do it.

Though it is a labor of love for which she is not paid, her book, *The God Box*, witnesses the Spirit-filled culmination of her life as a professional Christian minister thus far. As the song says, "I just can't keep from singing," Lynn just can't keep from ministering. It is who she is, who she has become.

One would hope that we have moved beyond the sort of thinking that would say, "Oh, the *The God Box*, what a cute idea, a pious little book on prayer, just the sort of thing a woman might do." *The God Box* is the mature work of an experienced minister who has honed her skills and her theology for almost four decades of church work, occasioned by her own struggle with cancer and written at the height of her powers. She tackles the tough theological issues surrounding prayer in our postmodern world: Is it realistic to pray? Does prayer really work? Should we be praying for miracles? How can we tell if our prayers are answered? And in the process of addressing those thorny issues, Lynn Neu, in *The God Box*, gives the reader a kaleidoscopic picture of suffering humanity as well as the basic principles of a "theology of suffering" and the importance of forming "community."

In my estimation, *The God Box* is a substantial book not to be read hurriedly. One should read a chapter and then let it meld in your soul for a bit before moving on to the next chapter. That way, one will better receive and assimilate the inherent "wisdom" of Lynn Neu's latest ministerial achievement—*The God Box*.

Dick Westley
Emeritus Professor
Loyola University–Chicago

Acknowledgements

"Having someone to regard the world with" is number 6 on a list of *Ten Good Reasons to be Married.* "Someone who I can laugh and cry with about what is happening to us." Someone who shares "a dual ringside seat on life where, as the years go by, the understanding takes on new depth."[1] This someone for me is Jerry. From first news that I could have cancer, through surgery and chemotherapy, Jerry held me close and calmed my fears. He gathered up my hair as fast as it fell out, stopped everything at 3:00 p.m. each day after surgery to eat popsicles and watch the Ellen Degeneres Show with me, and sang and prayed me to sleep each night with Healing Touch. He read everything we could get our hands on about ovarian cancer and went to every doctor's appointment and treatment with me. He lavished me with humor and understanding, compassion and hope, tenderness and care. To say I love this man is understatement. To say I am grateful only scratches the surface.

Julie and David are the sweetest gifts of my marriage to their father. During chemo, it was Julie who, in the midst of her own suffering, called me again and again to listen to everything I was going through. Hers was deep listening, the kind that bears the scars of having been there. Suffering builds a bridge. My suffering, and hers, has brought us closer. Humble gratitude fills my heart.

David and his darling wife, Espy, were bridges too. Their generosity afforded mountaintop and seaside retreats that opened me wide to write. Despite their whirlwind schedules, they were always there with tender care, bold encouragement, and the Belleruth Naparstek CD that helped keep my mind in the game.

My mom and dad, Nana and Pops as they became known, were the first to put me in touch with love of God and love of one another. They taught me how to pray and laugh and love broadly and deeply. They provided the foundation on which everything I am and do is built. I love them so much and I miss them deeply.

Steve Le Mere, dear and only brother of mine, toughened me up and lightened me up with all his teasing and kidding. Much to my sadness, he didn't live to see *The God Box* come to press, but I know that he helped bring it to completion. How I miss hearing "Hey, Lynneeeeeee! How are ya?" as he commuted to work with me by cell phone each week. I love you, Pissy! This one's for you.

Diana, Andrea, Brandon, and Milan, along with granddaughters, Danielle and Alex, complete my immediate family. We do life together through laughter and tears. Family, this family, is the glue that holds things together.

Then there are the others—so many generous souls who have given their time, their resources, and their wisdom to bring *The God Box* to life. I am grateful beyond telling to

- Dick and Joanne Woelfel, cheerleaders and entertainers extraordinaire, who open their home and their hearts to us and all our friends each time we "go home" to Racine. Our journey with Dick through his wife Kathy's death provided early schooling in suffering, persistence, faith, and devotion and helped us know we weren't wrong to pray for a miracle.

- Mimi and Allen Munro, who kept poking us to get away to their condos in Colorado so I could write. They finally convinced me, and the time there proved most fruitful of all!

- Annie Rimkus and Marilyn Ladwig, best friends throughout life who shared everything, even cancer. Marilyn, I miss you. Annie, thank God you survived!

- Ginny and David Burnight, closest "couple" friends, who shared my excitement or whatever else I was feeling every step of the way and encouraged me to keep going.

- Dick Westley, favorite professor, who presented and lived the reign of God so vividly that it ignited my own passion and desire to go and do likewise. Thanks for reading my book and writing the foreword in just one weekend!

- my cousin, Steve Mariotti, who suggested calling this *The God Box.* And for his wife, Sharon, whose idea it was in the first place!

- my Wisdom Circle who helped make this a better book: Andrew Ashbacher, Ginny Burnight, Dominic DeLay, Martha Garcia, Nancy Hatch, Tom Heywood, Gertrud Mueller Nelson, Maureen Nichols, and Chris Witt.

- my spunky, creative, Spirit-filled friend JanetMarie Colby for her imaginative God Box illustrations that decorate these pages.

- my boss, Father John Paul Forte, who held me in an easy balance of work and rest as I went through surgery and treatment for cancer. Thanks for knowing the value of a sabbatical and encouraging me to take the time to write.

- my colleagues at the Catholic Community at UCSD who covered for me while I was recovering and while I was away for sabbatical: Father JP, Patty Stewart, Julie Marner, Father Dominic DeLay. And to all those generous volunteers who came to their assistance!

- my massage, Reiki and Healing Touch angels who soothed my body, mind, and spirit and helped me heal: Judy Deken, Ellyn Hartman, Barb and Dick Mauro, Cherie Herrera, Hope Moore.

- Drs. David Chang, Perry Wittgrove, Albert Pisani, Steven Kossman, Ronald Goldberg, Cheryl Saenz—all responsible in some way for keeping me alive! Thanks for your incredible skill, dedication, and care.

- all those who supported this effort financially. I am humbled by your generosity. And so grateful that you believed in me and in this book.

- the God Box Community whose lives are woven into this text and who provide a dynamic example of a virtual community of loving kindness. You gave me hope, strength, and courage when I needed them most!

Open Up the Box!

1

The Story behind the God Box

But first, the story behind God. Whenever I think of God, I think of Jesus. Jesus is the way I have gotten to know who God is and how God does. Jesus is the one who is always on the side of those who are on the edge—the sick, the dying, the weak, the poor, the underdog, the underrepresented, the undocumented, the unofficial. Jesus binds up, makes whole, heals, delivers, reconciles, cures, loves, embraces, seeks, finds, holds, endears, cheers. Jesus is the one who makes the first move, shows up, stands by, resides with, believes in, forgives. Limitless love and limitless understanding. That's the Jesus I know. That's the God I believe in.

When I found out that I probably had ovarian cancer, that I could die sooner rather than later, this is the story of God I needed to hang on to. This is the God I needed to talk to. But first, I had to pack my bags and get to the beach. My husband and I had been planning for weeks to go there for our traditional anniversary getaway. Of course, we wondered, *should we go?* Then we decided, *how could we not?* What if time, *my* time, were suddenly cut short? Wouldn't we be glad that we didn't miss the chance to celebrate life while we still had the chance? Wouldn't going to the beach be more life-giving than staying home in the darkness of our fear?

With this news rattling inside us, we began to pack. Within hours, we were at our favorite seaside resort, watching the sun set, toasting twenty-seven years of marriage through tears, and counting down to radical surgery the next week. Fearing our future, we wondered whether or not we'd get back to this magical place the following year to celebrate number 28.

Everything had changed, and yet nothing had changed. It was all there: the dinner, the red wine, the soft music, the sound of the waves. And *we* were there, sort of. We were there, but we were distracted, preoccupied, scared. We were there and not there at the same time. Living in the present was more difficult than usual.

Later, not knowing what more to say, unable to sleep, I lay on my back in the dark, in the thick silence, with my hands on my belly. I breathed deeply and began talking with my friend, the Healer—Jesus, the Miracle Worker. I found comfort in reciting, like a litany, all the ways I had come to know him. I named every characteristic I could think of. Then I recalled all the ways I knew he had healed others—the blind man, the hemorrhaging woman, the paralyzed man, the Samaritan woman. I remembered that he even brought Lazarus back *from death,* which reminded me of John Shea's insight that in that story, Jesus was saying, *"I can bring life out of anything."*

As I lay there in the dark with Jerry, yet alone, I heard myself saying, *Jesus, I know you can do this. I know you have done this for others. I know you like to be asked. So I'm asking, please heal me. Yes, I've been skeptical about miracles. I never quite know what to make of Lourdes, but I've never not trusted that you have power to heal. And so I am asking you, please heal me. I know you can do this. I know I need to participate. I'll do my part. Promise.*

I prayed my way through the night and talked and cried my way through the weekend. And when I got home, I wrote emails. My gut instinct was to tell everyone I knew that I might have cancer. I know this is not everyone's initial reaction to personal illness, but it was mine. I asked my friends and colleagues to pray with me . . . *for me*. One of my old professors emailed back with "Oh no, not you!" in the subject line. This from the "Death and Dying" professor who had us read Ernest Becker's *The Denial of Death* for his class! Any trace of denial morphed quickly into shock. That one little line in the subject box of an email hit me right between the eyes. Yes, this is about me, and yes, this is serious. I'm going to need all the help I can get.

I had heard of prayer "warriors," but violent language doesn't work for an aspiring pacifist. *Partners* . . . I needed *partners*. I needed people to be with me, people who could encourage me, calm me, cheer for me, hope with me.

One email led to another. After surgery, soon as I was able to sit up at the computer long enough to plunk out a few sentences, I wrote to my "prayer partners" and told them I had late-stage ovarian cancer—3B—just short of being in my lymph nodes. The good news was that the surgeon had gotten it all. I thanked them and I thanked God. I shared the poem that sprang to my lips the day after surgery as I walked my IV stand around the halls. The poem is one I memorized in college. It's by E. E. Cummings:

> i thank You God for most this amazing
> day: for the leaping greenly spirits of trees
> and a blue true dream of sky; and for everything
> which is natural which is infinite which is yes
>
> (i who have died am alive again today,
> and this is the sun's birthday; this is the birth
> day of life and of love and wings: and of the gay
> great happening illimitably earth)
>
> how should tasting touching hearing seeing
> breathing any—lifted from the no
> of all nothing—human merely being
> doubt unimaginable You?
>
> (now the ears of my ears awake and
> now the eyes of my eyes are opened)

Inspiring thoughts buried in memory rise up when the situation calls for them. They are trusted friends riding just beneath the surface who can show up on a moment's notice. I was grateful for E. E. Cummings's words that broke through that morning after the day before, and grateful that someone taught me to memorize poetry.

Upon receiving my post surgery email, my prayer partners wrote back one after the other. I made regular trips to my computer throughout the day, every day, to lap up their words of encouragement, their expressions of faith, their hope, and their huge doses of love. I was surrounded with life-sustaining, positive energy. How could I do anything but heal?

As the initial shock that I had cancer wore off, fear, anxiety, and insecurity were waiting in the wings. I needed to trust in ways I had never been pushed to trust before. I needed to find a secure place to dwell. I found God's tent. I found it in the Psalms, in my husband, and in my prayer partners. There were many tears in the first week after surgery. Tears of sadness for what I was losing, tears of joy for all the love around me, tears releasing the tension of not knowing exactly what I faced, tears of gratitude for God's consistent, dependable love, tears of letting go.

In the midst of all those tears, I invited my prayer partners into God's tent—the one I found in a contemporary version of Psalm 27:

> For I shall hide in Love's heart
> in the day of trouble,
> As in a tent in the desert,
> Away from the noise of my fears.
> And I shall rise above
> my struggles and pain,
> Shouting blessings of gratitude
> in Love's Heart

As the days went on, my trust grew. A line from twelfth-century mystic Julian of Norwich became my mantra: "All shall be well, and all shall be well, and all manner of things shall be well." Safe in my tent in the desert of cancer, I relaxed in the arms of a loving God and a loving community and began the work of healing.

My prayer partners took tremendous interest in me. In fact, their interest is the one thing that remains the most amazing gift of cancer. My *being* was of interest to them. I could tell by the way they spoke. I could see it in their eyes when we met. I could feel it as I read their emails and cards and received all sorts of quilted comforts. Pure gift—unexpected, surprising in its intensity, delightful.

With encouragement from my prayer partners, my energy to write intensified. I told them all about the procedures, what "my numbers" were, how I was feeling, and how I was dealing with it all. At first, I wondered, *Why would anyone want to know all this? Too much information! I shouldn't write so much or so often. I'm imposing on their goodness.* But as soon as I hit the Send key, the responses would come flying back to my inbox. More love, more encouragement, more life-sustaining affection. I loved it! Who wouldn't? My spirits were buoyed up once again. I was not alone. I had the greatest cheerleaders on earth!

Six rounds of chemo came and went, and things looked good. People remarked that I seemed to skate through cancer. I raise my eyebrows at that, but I do remember thinking that cancer was not as bad as I thought it would be. It got my attention, but it didn't get me. Not everyone is so lucky. In the end, my numbers were perfect, the CAT scan was clear, and my hair was growing back. I had earned the big *R*. I was in remission. I shouted it to the world, once again through email: I'm alive! I, who have died, am alive again today! And the world shouted back, *Yoo-hoo!* We did it! OK, more accurately, more humbly, *God* did it!

I was just beginning to realize that it was probably time to cut the umbilical cord from this life-giving network when one of my prayer partners wrote back and said, "My friend is sick and needs our prayers. Your prayer partners are so powerful. Look what they did for you. Do you think you could ask them to pray for my friend?"

I felt a little like I might be imposing, but I wrote anyway and asked my prayer partners to pray for someone else—someone they didn't even know. And like clockwork, the responses came back, *"But of course!"*

The next day, another request came in. I sent it out, and the prayer partners sent it up like incense. Another day, another request. I sent it out, and the prayer partners sent it up. After a few more rounds of this, I feared I had created a monster. They must be growing tired of me, tired of the requests, and tired of getting too much email!

That's when my cousin Steve wrote and said that he has a box he calls his God Box where he puts the names of all the people who have asked for his prayers. He figures that he can't keep track of everyone, but he knows that's no problem for God. So he just puts the names in the box and then prays for "everyone in the God Box." I immediately shared this idea with my prayer partners and promised them I would send just *one* email per week rather than one a day, if that seemed OK. The God Box was born!

Prayer requests have been coming in ever since at the rate of ten to twenty per week. I keep gathering the needs and sending them off to an ever-growing list of participants. Friends of friends have a need, hear about the God Box, and want in. They are added to the list. Currently, there are close to five hundred people receiving the God Box each week.

The God Box has become a virtual community of loving kindness. It has become a place to witness the faith and struggles of others; a place to do a reality check about what's important in life; a laboratory in which we learn from each other how to pray, how to surrender, how to hope, how to grieve, how to celebrate life, how to be community in a world of individuals.

Through the chapters of this little book, I offer the God Box as a possibility. Perhaps you will see the benefit being more connected to the needs of others. Perhaps you will find ways to endure your own pain, your own suffering. Perhaps you will share those ideas, and they will become a source of healing for someone else. Perhaps your own vulnerability will encourage another's. Perhaps you will come to know deep down inside that you are loved, cared for, held close. Perhaps if your God is too small, God will get bigger for you. Perhaps you will be inspired to pray more. Perhaps you will become bolder in what you ask, how you ask, who you ask. Perhaps you will create your own God Box community.

"I tell you, ask and you will receive; seek and you will find; knock and the door will be opened to you" (Lk 11:9). The God Box Community keeps knocking. In gratitude and in hope, I help them connect to a network of other door-knockers. Together we knock on God's door, never sure what the answer will be, but trusting that somehow *all shall be well*. Won't you join us?

Lynn's first email, August 14, 2004:
Hi Everyone . . . My turn for prayers. I will be going in for a hysterectomy on Aug. 25 and would love to have your prayers guiding the surgeon's hands and keeping me safe. I have a rather large tumor that has benign characteristics . . . only the biopsy will tell for sure . . . but the odds are in my favor, I'm told. So . . . please keep me in your prayers.

And then, a couple of days later, August 18, 2004:
More news . . . not so reassuring. I got the result of the CA125 blood test for ovarian cancer today, and the numbers are way off what they should be. They don't like to see numbers higher than 35 and mine is 6300 . . . it reaffirms my need for surgery, and it will somewhat alter the course I'm on. I will now meet with a gynecologic oncologist on Monday for a pre-op consultation. I will undergo a complete hysterectomy, and they will do biopsies on everything in sight.

Yes, I am scared, but I am very glad to have such an incredible group of friends and family out there who are surrounding me with love and prayers and strength. A friend of mine told me yesterday that she didn't know what to say . . . that she just doesn't know what it feels like to be in my shoes. I told her I'm not sure I know what it feels like to be in my shoes! . . . I pray for courage and trust that all will be well.

Meanwhile, Jerry and I will go to Laguna Beach today as planned to celebrate our 27th anniversary. We will enjoy the sunset from my niece Andrea's boyfriend's balcony with some good hors d'oeuvres and red wine. Ahhh . . . this day . . . now . . . is where I will plant myself. Keep reminding me of that, OK?

I invite assistance from my friends and loved ones — past, present, future — to lend me their support and strength. I see myself surrounded by their love and caring, and I feel it all over my body like a warm wave.[2]

—Belleruth Naparstek

2

What Is a God Box Anyway?

It's a funny name to call the sacred receptacle of people's greatest needs and longings. Sanctuary or tabernacle or ark or perhaps something as simple as "prayer box" seems better suited, less *cute*. But "God Box" was offered at the outset of this phenomenon's development, and it has stuck. The idea of putting things into a container with God's name on it, having God's memory take care of things we can't remember, or God's strength holding things that have become too burdensome seemed like a good idea. But not everyone liked the *name*!

My friend Erika wrote to me and said, "I love my box, but from day one I had very ambivalent feelings about the name of this object, and I still harbor pretty much these same feelings. Yet in one sense I've undergone some sort of acceptance. I'm no longer quite as uptight when making use of the words *God Box.*"

Containers for prayers aren't new. God Boxes aren't new. A simple Internet search shows a great variety. God Boxes are actually quite popular, particularly with Alcoholics Anonymous and other twelve-step groups. Online, you can order wooden boxes, leather-lined, with fifteen coats of lacquer on the outside! The God Box is used as part of AA's twelve-step decision to turn your life over to a higher power, to surrender. If you go to Amazon.com, click on "Jewelry and Watches" and type "Prayer Boxes" in the search box, you will find many attractive silver boxes to wear around your neck on a cord or chain.

Recently, my friend Paula was wearing such a box around her neck. I could see a slip of paper inside the tiny filigreed box. She had just lost her husband. She was stepping back out into the world alone, in need of loving kindness, in need of strength and courage. I'm not sure what was written on the paper inside her little box, but I imagine it held her husband's name and carried, as well, her own grief, her own sadness, and her hope that all would be well as she entered this scary middle time between death and new life. She had surrendered her dear husband to God and was now surrendering herself to the grieving process and to her faith community. The God Box around her neck was somehow a symbol of all that.

As I began writing this book, my dear friend Anne, in a sweet gesture of support, gave me a beautiful cylindrical God Box on a chain. She told me that since the long lists I send out each week would not fit in this tiny cylinder, I could simply breathe my prayers into it. I like the idea of breathing each week's intentions into this little container. It reminds me of God's breath, *ruah,* breathing life into everything, breathing life into all those whose intentions I carry in my heart and, symbolically, in the little box around my neck. I love that it looks like a mezuzah, that little receptacle Jews post on their doorposts or wear around their neck containing the Shema, the line from Deuteronomy 6:4 proclaiming the oneness of God: "Hear, O Israel! The Lord is our God, the Lord alone." God is one, and we are one as we pray for each other.

Whether worn around the neck, lacquered fifteen layers deep, displayed prominently at home, kept in a sacred space, or stored in a computer or in a binder, the God Box is a receptacle for burdens—a place to put worry, fear, angst, and yes, even hope.

Anne Lamott helped me get over the notion of the God Box being cute. This no-nonsense, straightforward, "nothing-cute-about-her" kind of woman has a God Box. She writes about it in her column in *Salon* magazine.

> Eventually I am too tired to continue and my head has become too uninhabitable, and I realize I've been driving this rickety temperamental old bus of my mind around for too long. I've lost all sense of direction and am feeling confused and pissed off and bitter and resentful and

nuts; but then finally, finally just tired. I begin to worry that I have had or am having a complete nervous breakdown, and that I am about to start weeping or barking and won't be able to stop.

This is the point at which I am willing to try using a God-box, because, as is often true in life, the willingness comes from the pain.

I don't understand why it would hurt so much if just once in His life, [God] used a megaphone. But He never does. I find this infuriating. But what happens when I put a note in the God-box is that the phone rings, or the mail comes; and I hear from Him that way. [3]

Somehow, putting our problems into words and putting those words on the altar or in the God Box helps us to let go. We can stop wringing our hands. We can stop lugging our burden around with us wherever we go. We can hand our problem over, trusting we're in good hands.

Most of the God Boxes that I've discovered are meant for personal use. Individuals place their own need in their own box and give it over to their own God. That's a good and helpful thing, worth doing. It calls for surrender. It calls up trust. It's a place to stash secrets, hopes, concerns, dreams.

The God Box experience, of which I write, however, adds another dimension: community—a *virtual* community. *Virtual* here does not mean "almost real." It refers to an online, Internet, cyberspace community that connects people to one another easily and quickly in this fast-paced world. It is not a substitute for person-to-person contact, but a support for that. Through the God Box, individuals are invited not only to place their need in God's box, but in each other's box as well.

We are not alone. We are connected to one another. Once we tell others about our need, we invite their care, support, and loving kindness. As we watch each other ask for help, we become bolder with our own requests, less afraid of our own vulnerability. It's comforting to know that faithful people are committed to come to our rescue when called upon; that faithful people will share our burden, take it into themselves, and in some mysterious way, transform it.

This reminds me of something Ron Rolheiser once said about Jesus—how he received fear, held it, transformed it, and gave back freedom; how he took in chaos, held it, transformed it, and gave back order.[4] The virtual community that has formed around the God Box does just that. We hold each other's needs; transform them through the power of prayer; and give back to one another peace, courage, and a sense that all will be well. We participate in the saving power of God. Those in need breathe more easily, knowing that others are with them. God's presence is more tangible. "I am with you" resounds in our hearts as we are held in each other's.

"Some people can create lives of holiness all by themselves, the way Mozart could create immortal music without taking piano lessons, but most of us need a structure and the company of other people to do it."[5]

Involving others, though, can be scary. It's one thing for God to know our inmost thoughts, fears, and needs. It's quite another to say those things out loud to others or put them out on the Internet for all to see.

Surrender takes courage. As Anne Lamott so honestly demonstrates, getting to the box with our intention isn't always a slam dunk. Whether our box is our personal business or is shared with others, letting go is a challenge. Usually the pain has to get bad enough, or we have to get tired enough of carrying around that great big rock of concern all by ourselves. Anne Lamott shows us that it's all about "dropping the rock."

> This group of Hawaiian drunks had a meeting whose topic was about the 3rd Step, about letting go, and the name of this meeting was Drop the Rock. The Drop the Rock meeting was based on the understanding that left to our own devices, we—as a species—tend to lug these big rocks around. They are the rocks of our concerns. Everytime we get up, we reach down for our big rock and then we lug it out the door, down the stairs, and roll it into the back seats of our cars. Then after we drive someplace, we open the back door, get

out our rock, and carry it with us, wherever we go. Because it's our rock. It is very important to us and we need to keep it in sight. Also, someone could steal it.

So these Hawaii drunks suggest that you practice dropping the rock. That you put it down, on the ground at your feet. And that you say to God, to Mary, to Pele, Jehovah, Jesus, or Howard: "Here. I'm giving you the rock. YOU deal with it."

I realized that more than anything, I wanted to put down my rock. My psychic arms ached from carrying it. I got my note out of the God-box, and I re-read it, and then I folded it back up and said to God, "Here. Look at me—I am putting down the rock. It's in your hands now." RSVP.[6]

That's what people do when they put their request in the *God Box.* They drop their rock. They let go—at least a little—of fear and anxiety and the need to control what seems so out of control. They open themselves up to the loving kindness of others, and through that kindness, they often experience the graciousness of God. As a container for their intentions, the God Box becomes a sacred object, a sacramental—something material that holds something sacred. It stands as a testimony to trust and to loving kindness.

For everyone who asks, receives; and the one who seeks, finds; and to the one who knocks, the door will be opened. (Lk 11:10)

What does your box look like?
The God Box Community responds.

❖ Mine is a five-and-a-half-by-five-and-a-half-inch square wooden box with a decorated hinged lid. This beautiful box is two and a half inches high and was given to me as a housewarming present at the beginning of this year by a very dear friend. The necessary instructions of how to use the box were given to me by her in person. Needless to say, the box has a permanent and honored place in my home. In this box, many tiny folded pieces of paper come to rest. On all of them, on one side, a handwritten prayer petition: for family, friends, myself, and/or for prayer requests which come my way for people unknown to me.

❖ When I print out the God Box list, I cut out the names and then put it in a beautiful open wooden container I bought from a gentleman who does woodworking. It's not really a "box" as it is circular and has a woven pattern made by the wooden strips he used.

❖ For Christmas, I got my wife a jeweled box from Pier 1. I included candles and created special prayer-request cards to help God keep track of all those in the God Box!

❖ Sometimes, just seeing the box or being in its proximity prompts me to remember the heavy duty it contains. But the feeling, which the box projects—or which I project unto the box—is one of peace, warmth, solace, refuge. It's a mysterious happy feeling. Should you ever open my box, you would read on the inside of the lid Psalm 27: "For I shall hide in Love's heart."

❖ Even though this is called the "God Box," I don't copy all the requests and put them in a box. All I do is read them all and say a prayer that all of the intentions are included in a special way with the "liturgical and extraliturgical" acts I perform during each day of living out God's plan.

❖ While I'm away from home, my God Box is kept on my computer so I can remember everyone as I fire it up every day.

❖ At the last couple's retreat that Paul and I facilitated, I invited all those present to write on small sheets of paper the names of people that they were particularly concerned about and who they felt were competing for their energy and their time. We were all well aware that when people come to a retreat, especially couples, they leave behind children, grandchildren, friends, and relatives who put many demands on their time and in the concerns of their heart. It was a powerful moment when, in silence, they wrote the names of their beloved and then one by one entrusted them into the care and healing power of God, putting them in the sacred God Box. By doing so, they were relieving themselves of the burdens they carried so that they could be fully present to the special time they wanted to give themselves for their own healing and their own encounter with the Spirit of the Living God. We began each morning by lifting up the God Box in prayer for all the people in our lives and by thanking God for watching over our loved ones. All weekend long, the God Box kept being filled as people remembered more and more concerns. We finished again on the last day by raising the God Box in love and gratitude for the work of God in the lives of all our loved ones. The God Box was a beautiful tool that allowed people to unburden themselves and entrust their worries to a Higher Power. It freed them to be more present and attentive to the stirrings of the Holy Spirit within and around them. Paul and I gave each couple a small wooden box (lovely, made in India, and it only cost us one dollar each at Target). The couples who had been very moved by our collective box loved taking their own home.

❖ At a women's retreat, I gave each of the fifty women one simple white cardboard box. They loved receiving it, and they have often commented since that they are still using it. It was a visible way to keep the practice. I recommended that they get a bigger box in time. This is such a simple and beautiful way to keep our prayers visible on our own home altar!

❖ When I lived in Aruba as a child, a Dutch Dominican priest told how his mother in Holland had a cloth bag slung over a kitchen chair. She'd put birth announcements, wedding invitations, obituaries, etc., in the cloth bag. Each night, the family prayed the rosary after dinner. As his mother announced the mysteries of the rosary, she'd often say, "And this one's for the bag!" Reminds me of your God Box!

Kika's Story

My encounter with the God Box, in the beginning, was merely circumstantial and part of a tragic event in my life—the loss of my mother.

I knew little of my mother's routine in the last year of her life, but in various visits, I came to realize that she meditated upon waking. Sometimes she would get up before anyone else so she could sit quietly in her office. I knew enough to respect this time. I never liked to ask too many questions. I knew my mother was a very private person, and that she disliked it when we would pry. But I also realized just how unaware I was of her journey and what it entailed for her.

Shortly after her death, I found a small cardboard box in her office with a little red heart pasted on top. Feeling ashamed, as though I was intruding, I opened this little box. Curiosity got the better of me. Inside, I found tiny pieces of paper folded up. Still feeling ashamed, I gently unfolded a few that were inside and then realized that they were prayers. Now I truly felt as though I had intruded. I folded the prayers and put them back into the little box and returned it to its original place of rest. I then shared this with my brother. It is important to mention that, for us, those initial days in her apartment was like being on a tour of discovering who our mother was.

In her office she had a bookcase with a handcrafted cloth draped over it, and on top, a flower vase as well as figurines she held dear—things she had received as gifts from friends and family. She had also placed a candle in a jar and a tapered candle resting in a bed of rice. This was next to another box that was also gently covered with a white hand-embroidered napkin. On top of this box rested a handcrafted wooden angel.

Curiosity continued to get the better of me as I proceeded to discover what I later would realize was her "God Box." Weeks later, while going through her computer, I discovered the God Box prayer group. Then I discovered something that she wrote entitled "Confessions of a God Box User." And then it all came together for me. I needed to be a part of this.

In moments of uncertainty and desperation and what I would call a series of events, I began to participate in the God Box, seeking comfort in difficult times. I have to admit that I faithfully look forward to Mondays and to the contents of the week's intentions. Not a Monday goes by that, when reading the intentions, tears don't flow as I contemplate the difficulties that others are encountering. Somehow my difficulties just seem so trivial, and I reflect then on what I should be grateful for.

We participate and live in a society today where we are more and more isolated from each other, each one of us leading very hurried isolated lives, between work, engagements, obligations, family, etc. The God Box provides the feeling that there is someone out there who cares. Besides that, Lynn's own personal stories allow each one of us to peer through a window where we can see and feel who she is. She is able to share with us a positive attitude, enthusiasm, and most importantly, joy and happiness.

3

Becoming a Virtual Community of Loving Kindness

I was surprised by the blank expression on a young guy's face when I shared Leonard Sweet's insight from *SoulTsunami* that the Internet has become the white picket fence of our day. It made perfect sense to me, but I could tell there were no lights going on for this guy. "What's a white picket fence?" he finally asked. He didn't have a clue.

Stunned by our generation gap, I patiently described the quaint white paint-sucking wooden slat fence that adorned many a front or backyard "in the days when." It's what people used to talk over. Even with a phone in every house, it was more typical to chat with neighbors over the fence than over the phone.

In those days, people talked to people rather than to screens, across fences rather than across cyberspace. In those days, people stopped by the house for coffee or dessert or just to say "hi" the same way people today stop by their email to check in with each other. The difference, however, is that today, the yard next door can be any place around the globe; you can reach it any time of day or night without imposing, and people tend to visit much more frequently. You can check email while you're on the phone, in class, or at a meeting without appearing rude—at least until you're caught! Today, thanks to email, you can get in and out of a conversation quickly, have a record of your conversation, talk to several people at the same time, and conserve precious time as you go. It's fast, efficient, and far-reaching. And it's shaping the way we do community.

I'm not sure we used the word "community" to describe what we experienced in those old neighborhoods, but we knew that's what we had. We experienced community in families that ate together, congregations that prayed together, and in real letters that arrived after a few days' journey via "snail mail." We enjoyed real live face-to-face encounters rather than Myspace or Facebook encounters. No one had ever heard of a virtual community.

I was surprised that my young friend did not know what a white picket fence was, but I am not surprised when I see question marks on the faces of baby boomers or those from "the greatest generation" when I use the words "virtual community" to describe the God Box experience. Some have the impression that a virtual community is an *almost* community. A few confuse it with virtual reality, a computer simulation of a 3-D environment that makes you feel like you are really there.

Virtual communities are neither *almost* nor *simulated.* They are groups of people linked by common interests or concerns and computer technology. *Wikipedia* describes a virtual/online community as "a group of people that primarily or initially communicates or interacts via the Internet rather than face-to-face. Online communities have also become a supplemental form of communication between people who know each other in real life." For those who aren't there yet, welcome to postmodern culture! For those who swim easily in this culture, be patient with the rest who are paddling along behind you!

There are thousands of virtual communities. Howard Rheingold is credited with inventing the term in a book he wrote in 1993 entitled *The Virtual Community.*[7] In it, he lists forty examples from hundreds of separate topics available from just *one* organization called the Parenting Conference—everything from "New Well Baby," to "Kids and Death," to "All the Poop on Diapers"! There is virtually no end to the number of topics or groups out there in cyberspace. Where there's a concern or need, there's a group.

Religious organizations are tiptoeing their way into this new technology. Sites like Beliefnet.com and Gratefulness.org lead the way. There's fear, of course, that online relationships and communities could keep us from personal interaction; current research shows otherwise. According to the Pew Internet and American Life Project, "email does not seduce people away from in-person and phone contact . . . People use the Internet to put their social networks into motion when they need help with important issues in their lives."[8] Pew research also discovered that faith-related activity online is a supplement to, rather than a substitute for, offline religious life and that Internet activity supplements their ties to traditional institutions, rather than moving them away from church.[9]

Virtual communities seem to stimulate a desire for personal contact rather than detract from it. Virtual communities most often intensify relationships that already exist and make connections where none existed before.

I hadn't really thought of creating a virtual community when I started sending emails to family and friends about my cancer diagnosis. I just knew I needed prayer and support, and I needed it right away. No time or energy to call everyone. No need or desire to talk to everyone. I simply wanted to connect. I wanted people to know what was happening to me. I needed them at my side even though they are scattered all over the world. Virtually at my side or physically at my side, it didn't matter. I just couldn't carry the burden of cancer alone. I did what the Pew research project found people doing. I used the Internet to put my social network into motion.

I raked through my email address book looking for people who pray. I created a list and labeled it Prayer Partners. It included family members, close friends, colleagues, and the nuns I love—a whole Dominican community of seasoned prayers! Within my community, there were little sub communities—friends who knew friends, colleagues who'd worked together, former students, fellow retreatants, travelers, and learners from various periods of my life. I mixed them all together to create the combustible energy force I needed to fight cancer. It was like hearing the *wa-woomph* sound of a gas grill or fireplace igniting as I sent off those first emails.

Besides the personal list I had created, I wanted to include people from the Catholic community at UCSD where I worked. Many of them see each other Sunday after Sunday and have known each other for years. Some are now separated by distance or circumstance, yet they continue to stay connected through a Yahoo! group. With the stroke of a key, I could send my note to an additional three hundred people who I knew would join the chorus, letting their prayers rise up like incense, sending smoke signals to God in my name. *Wa-woomph!* I felt better already!

I felt even better when cards began to arrive, when people called or stopped by to chat, or whenever I was *with* my community. The Internet never took the place of these wonderful people or their personal acts of loving kindness. The Internet could never dole out hugs the way my friends and family could. With one hundred unique smiley faces available online to decorate email, there is still nothing quite as beautiful as someone's smile from across the room. The Internet helped me get the word out; *people* brought love to my door. Of course, not everyone could literally come to my door. Some live far away, and we would not be seeing each other anytime soon. The Internet would bridge the gap until we did. In the meantime, I relished every word and every blessing delivered to my inbox from the folks next door and from friends as far away as France and Japan.

When it was time to go to the hospital for surgery, I had a whole stack of emails generated by my cry for help. I printed them out so I could see them all in a pile and keep them as a visible reminder of how many people were out there praying for me. I three-hole-punched them and put them in a big fat binder. They became my "messages to live by." Under the clear plastic binder cover, I placed the inspirational prayers people sent—among them, Thomas Merton's prayer about trusting God's will and the "Memorare" proclaiming Mother Mary's holy assistance. I propped that binder up against the wall at the end of my hospital bed as a point of focus. *Wa-woomph!* I'm going to be OK. As I walked my IV stand around the halls the day after surgery, thanking God for most this amazing day, I am sure my barely moving body was carried by the healing energy of so many faithful people's prayers. I thank you, God, for most this amazing day and for most this amazing Internet that has connected me to their loving kindness!

In the months following surgery, I continued to write and receive email. I shared my gratefulness for being alive, my admiration for my doctors, my delight in having such good friends, my renewed joie de vivre. I told people all about the treatments, my daily routines, my feelings, my faith in God, and my faith in them. In an attempt to give back to those holding me up in my time of need, I'd often pass on a prayer, a reflection, a quote, or notes from a retreat or conference that was meaningful to me.

Years ago, when I was teaching high school, I read something that has always stuck with me: "You know what you have given them; you do not know what they have received." So it was with my emails. I was frequently amazed at how something I wrote touched another person. Simply mentioning that I was off to the gym nudged someone to get off the couch! So I'm off to the gym today. Big deal. Yet somehow, that one little line spoke to someone, told them that care of the body is important, that how we fuel and tune and tend to our physical being matters. I knew not what they received. As I shared my faith and the prayers I love, others were encouraged to develop a deeper prayer life. As I lived through "what is" in my own life, others seemed to embrace their own situations with greater courage. Again, I knew not what they received until they told me. I simply wrote emails!

Embedded in those emails were a positive attitude and an inherent trust in God that all will be well. I grew up on that philosophy. I had exercised it for years; and now, without my knowing, it was flexing its muscle and encouraging others to get "positively" fit as well. I wanted everyone to know about God's goodness. I wanted everyone to know of their own goodness too and the positive effect that was having on me. As time went on, my prayer partners began witnessing their own powerful effect. I asked for their loving kindness, and they gave it. I asked for prayers for healing and felt lifted up by them. My prayer partners and I were experiencing the transformative power of prayer, the sustaining power of community, and the connection between faith, healing, and the Internet.

What began as my communication with a group of people who love and care for me grew into a virtual community of loving kindness for everyone involved. These people saw something happen to me. They watched me "skate" through cancer on the wings and prayers of a loving community. I may have been on thin ice, but the uplifting love, prayer, and action of the group kept me from falling through. Never before had I so deeply felt the importance of community and the power of prayer. Others were feeling it too and they wanted in! *Wa-woomph!* Energy exploded and the God Box was born.

Research shows that virtual communities intensify relationships and make connections where none existed before. That's what happened in the God Box. Just as I was ready to stop writing emails to everyone, something new burst forth. *Could you ask your powerful prayers to pray for my friend?* That was the beginning of my little virtual community, making connections where none existed before. People who didn't even know each other were interested in sharing the love. Those who did know each other were glad to learn the details of their friends' struggles so they could offer resources or greater care. They liked knowing more than a one-line intercessory prayer in church could hold. The God Box connected them more profoundly to one another, whether they saw each other every week, whether they were miles apart, or whether they had ever even met each other.

Andrew Weil says, "One of the most effective ways to neutralize medical pessimism is to find someone who had the same problem you do and is now healed."[10] There is something about attaching ourselves to people who have "made it." That helps us make it. When I was going through chemo, I wanted to touch my eighty-five-year-old friend, an eighteen-year survivor of ovarian cancer, the way you touch a good luck charm. I'd do high fives with her and hug her every chance I got. I wanted what she had—remission. Two years later, she experienced a recurrence and has since died. While she was undergoing treatment, she'd hug me and say, "Give me some!" Underneath that, I heard, "Give me the positive energy I need. Give me hope. Give me courage. Give me some!" It's what I also hear underneath requests for prayers that are submitted every week in the God Box.

David Steindl-Rast says that growth in faith means "learning to make the basic gesture of faith in more and more difficult circumstances, in circumstances in which the faithfulness to which faith responds is less and less obvious. In the end, we ought to be able to trust in that 'faithfulness at the heart of all things' even when we cannot see it at all."[11] It's hard for us when we cannot see for ourselves. Seeing faithfulness in someone else helps us. We take courage in their courage. Steindl-Rast says, "Every time we move another step, every time we repeat the inner gesture of courage and trust, we do not only exercise faith, we tap the very source of faithfulness that gives us strength to go on."[12]

Time and again, we see that happening in the God Box. We become witnesses to the faith of others, and it encourages our own. Each time someone asks for prayers, we experience a dependency on God and a need to be held by others that is not typical of our usual declaration of independence. When we see someone else say, "I am in need," that somehow releases us to say, "Me, too." As one person opens up their deepest need for healing or strength or patience or hope or guidance, we recognize our own need. We become more courageous ourselves and learn to make the gesture of faith in our own difficult circumstances.

In the God Box, we meet people who are scared, brave, anxious, open, vulnerable, hopeful, faithful, compassionate. We see the human condition played out before our eyes. Today you need me. Tomorrow I'll need you. Suffering is inevitable; we all get a turn. We are not alone.

One thing I learned from cancer is that we are dependent on God and one another more than we know. And the generosity of others is bigger than we ever imagine. We need to let ourselves receive what others have to offer. There are so many healing touches to be had if only we are open to them.

Life will teach us if we let it. Other people will teach us if we let them. In the God Box, we not only watch what each other is dealing with, we watch *how* each other deals as well. We see raw fear and a tremendous need for a place to park that fear for a while. We need what the tent in Psalm 27 speaks of—a place to hide. We need to be held in each other's strong arms as well as in God's and to know that we are "perfectly, utterly safe."[13]

Sometimes the pain and suffering we experience in the God Box becomes overwhelming. After a few months of receiving so many heavy-duty requests for prayer, David, a UCSD grad, wanted to lighten things up with some good news about the birth of his daughter. His response to seeing so much pain and suffering was gratitude for what he was given. It is the most common response of God Box participants. Gratefulness expands as we recognize the fragility of life, as we witness the tough times others are going through. Since David's first gratitude entry, I always begin the God Box by listing "This Week's Praise and Thanks." It is where participants share good news, give progress reports, tell how even though God's will was not their will, they are somehow at peace or at least experiencing some comfort.

From the beginning, I have spoken of the God Box community as a virtual community of loving kindness. Those words came to me without realizing how much they are used in both Buddhism and Judaism. In Buddhism, *"lovingkindness"* refers to extending goodwill, care, and consideration to all beings, without exception. Judaism speaks of thirteen attributes of *lovingkindness* that come from chapter 33 of the book of Exodus—attributes like realizing the divinity of self and the divinity of others, engendering compassion, finding grace, acting with equanimity, preserving kindness. Love and kindness are the heart and soul of Christianity though linking the two words as one seems to be more a Buddhist and Jewish thing. For Christians, love's attributes, epitomized by Jesus, show up in 1 Corinthians 13: "Love is patient; love is kind; love bears all things, believes all things, hopes all things, endures all things; love never fails." We've all heard it said that kindness begets kindness. It's true!

The loving kindness that I have experienced in the God Box has led me to reach out in bigger ways and without question, more than I used to. I find myself unable to resist writing, calling, visiting people who are sick or who are going through tough times. It's catching. I take time each week to send out the God Box, and I don't count the cost. It's what I do. And the faithful folk on my lists go at their work of praying just as easily. It's what they do. More than that, they reach out to one another with information, important connections, and their own stories of hope. They even ask about each other when no progress report is given. Each act of kindness evokes another. Each cry for help lets others know it's OK to cry out.

Loving kindness is a practice. Every time we open the God Box, we practice. We practice opening ourselves to one another. We practice holding pain until it can be transformed. And as we practice, we learn how prayer and loving kindness bring life to death, hope to despair, love to fear, calm to anger, freedom to anxiety. We *see* it happening. We are at the heart of life. We are sewing seeds of compassion and love. Buddhist monk, Thich Nhat Hanh, says that practices of loving kindness create true peace. And so they do.

For many, the God Box has created a sacred space in cyberspace. My friend G thinks of it as a contemporary cloister. In *this* cloister, there is no separation between prayer and living in the world. As we sit at our computers, we pause. We take time to remember that life is not just about what we can compute. There's a much-deeper mystery that rides beneath the surface. Suffering is a part of that mystery. Why one suffers and another does not defies explanation. In the God Box, we keep vigil with the mystery. We wait. We hope. We give thanks. Our email experience is transformed. We are no longer simply doing tasks of reading and writing, sending and receiving, hunting and finding.

Our computer routine has become a sort of liturgy of the hours as we dip in and out of work and prayer. The rhythm of our day changes a bit. We have room for others, even in the midst of projects and deadlines. Our concerns don't seem so singularly awful as we read and pray about our traveling companions who, this day, have bigger problems than we do. In the God Box, we sit in the school of mindfulness. Life doesn't just keep swirling. We stop. We see. We are with each other for a moment.

Sometimes when the God Box email arrives, there is no time to open it. Yet in the midst of a stressful day, there's a tug at our heartstrings to look at it anyway. We know there are people whose fight for time has nothing to do with meeting today's deadlines. The God Box stops us in our tracks. It tells us to slow down, to appreciate, to be happy now, to enjoy one another now. Our days will run out. Our time is measured. We have today. We recognize our own vulnerability as we sit with each other's grief or pain or difficulty. More than anything, we learn gratitude for this day, this time, this God-given life.

Touching the pain of another is like touching the Holy. There is something sacred about shared vulnerability, something that puts us in touch with the depths of another's being and connects us to our own. Vulnerability strips us of pretensions that camouflage our fears and hopes. Vulnerability exposes our dependence and celebrates our need for God and one another. In this naked space, we stand before the mystery of life, and we do what Jesus instructed us to do. We just ask.

After my fourth round of chemo, I went to a wedding. A whole group of UCSD grads had come from around the country. They knew all about my cancer journey through my emails. They were part of my virtual community. Someone took a picture, which I pasted to the front of my computer. Twenty times a day, at least, I would look at that picture. There I was—big smile; lovely wig; looking downright healthy; surrounded by a half-dozen bright, gracious, generous, loving grads. The caption beneath the picture? God's skin. Those grads were exactly that; they were God's holy, tangible presence holding me together. Every time I looked at them in that picture, I touched the face of God. When the chemo drugs lined up once again to attack any remaining cancer cells, God's skin protected me.

White picket fences aren't what they used to be. Neither are the screens we sit in front of. We've spent a lot of time worrying about how time spent at the computer can lead to isolation. There is that possibility; we must be careful. However, the potential for connection and for community is an even greater possibility. More and more people are using the Internet to connect with people over things that matter to them. More and more people are recognizing that cyberspace can become sacred space. Holy purposes like praying for one another and practicing loving kindness can happen through this wonderful worldwide web of communication. The God Box is but one example.

What's it like to be part of this virtual community?
The God Box Community responds.

❖ I find great inspiration from the God Box and the community that prays together. Although I have conflicts that keep me out of the church right now, I know how powerful a community can be in prayer. Your experience about your cancer and your openness helped me when I was diagnosed.

❖ I find the emails are a miniature representation of the human condition.

❖ I love being part of the God Box. It was actually very stabilizing for me to receive the God Box while I was in Japan. Praying for others across the world helped me to fill the church community void that I was missing while working in Japan.

❖ When I see a God Box message, it blesses my whole email experience. It's such a profound and different use of computer technology that it always gives me pause.

❖ I've become even more aware of the pain, which is experienced by most everyone at some point in their life. Simultaneously it has also clarified the fact for me that shared pain, anxiety, and concerns are tolerated with greater ease if they can be confided and communicated to others whose intentions are to help ease this pain with their own intercessory prayers.

❖ When I see real problems other people have, mine feel pretty small, and I'm suddenly feeling very grateful that mine are so meager.

❖ It is my escape from the daily business where I don't think I have time to pray . . . and then . . . as I am taking care of "business" in the computer . . . when I see the email God Box . . . all of a sudden there is room for God!

❖ Sometimes I don't get around to reading the intentions till the end of the week, but I read them all. It also depends what kind of mood I'm in. The God Box can be depressing sometimes because it reports so much pain/sickness/struggle that is overwhelming to read sometimes.

❖ The God Box gets me out of my own "stuff" and connects me to the powerful energy of prayer given so freely for "strangers." It certainly gives me more perspective and compassion for others!

❖ This God Box has been a way to keep informed of our community members who need that extra prayer at this time in their lives. I had been giving massages to someone for a while. She would just say she had so much stress. I accepted that and massaged away with good intentions. But after she wrote the piece about her son for the God Box, I was able to pray for her with much more compassion and earnestness. I appreciate her willingness to share her trials and ask for assistance. That takes courage.

❖ With the God Box, we feel we are participating in a wonderful group process that will help others. I am sure God is impressed.

❖ I feel some measure of guilt because I do not normally try to pray for the needs in the God Box, yet I hope that reading the God Box entries helps me to take actions that are more patient, loving, and kind than if I were not pulled out of the rush of daily life to witness, in a way, the hope and faithfulness of others.

❖ The God Box is a good start to the week. When I read about all the medical problems and hardships of the people in the God Box, it helps put my personal problems into perspective. It feels good to pray for others and know that I'm helping someone that I don't even know. In addition to praying for the God Boxers, I pray in thanksgiving that I am healthy and life is good. And if I do fall on hard times, it's comforting to know that I can call upon the support of the God Box.

❖ I think it has increased my gratitude, reminding me every day of the good things in my life—health, good kids, etc. And made me feel connected to lots of other people in their good times and bad.

❖ Friendship is God's special way of loving us through someone else. The God Box is a blessed extension of that friendship!

❖ Our family loves reading the God Box! It's a whole family experience! Just reading all of the prayers of gratitude and the prayers for healing, etc., is a spiritual experience in itself. It really has broadened ours and our children's view of the world. It is so easy for Moira and Fiona to see only their friends and family as needing our prayers. The God Box is a reminder that everyone needs prayers, that God loves us all.

❖ The God Box keeps me connected to friends and my spiritual home of eight years and provides inspiration, joy, and solace.

❖ It has been like adding another prayer time to my week. I am lifted up by the prayers of gratitude and humbled by the petitions. Reading about the serious problems so many people struggle with has helped me put my own little annoyances and challenges into perspective.

For many of us, at some point in the spiritual journey, the divine energy reaches a sort of tipping point, and a once-personal quest becomes more universal: The wounded become healers. The warriors, statesmen. The victims, advocates.

—Patricia Auberdene, *Megatrends, 2010*

A HOT (Hand On Technology) church will superconnect its people, stimulating and shaping an online community that is as vibrant and as vital as its physical community. A HOT church will take up the challenge of creating Christ-body communities in cyberspace and make the Web a gathering place for Christians.

—Leonard Sweet, *SoulTsunami*

Sometimes our light goes out, but is blown again into instant flame by an encounter with another human being. Each of us owes the deepest thanks to those who have rekindled this inner light.

—Albert Schweitzer

We are one, after all, you and I; together we suffer, together exist, and forever will recreate each other.

—Pierre Teilhard de Chardin

4

It's Hard to Type with a Sawed-off Finger!

Driving from one meeting to the next in rush hour traffic on a Friday night is probably not the best time to catch up on missed cell phone calls. I know that . . . I *tell* myself that. Then I usually pick up the phone and check my messages anyway. Just as I was merging on to the freeway that would take me back to the university, barely squeaking by between semi trucks and motorcycles, I picked up the first message. It was Andrew's mom telling me that he was in the hospital awaiting surgery, having nearly cut off his finger with an electric saw. That's where I almost went over the edge of the freeway.

Andrew is a college student whose energy and enthusiasm for life should be bottled and distributed freely throughout the world! Andrew is fearless. He climbs trees, leaps walls, jumps high, and skips through life. He's an Eagle Scout who is generous beyond telling. He has a milewide smile and a heart that burns to serve. Everybody loves Andrew.

I listened to the message again. "They hoped to save his finger," she said, "but it was a very nasty cut, with bone and tendon involved." The very thought of Andrew's mangled finger sent shivers right through me. My imagination did somersaults as his mom calmly reported what had happened. Then came the purpose of her call. Andrew had asked her to call so he could get his name in the God Box right away! Later, Andrew told me that there were three calls he needed to make when he knew he was in trouble: one to his mom, one to the priests, and one to me because as he said, "It's hard to type an email request to the God Box with a sawed-off finger!"

There was Andrew, in shock, holding the hand that played the guitar the day before, not knowing if he'd ever play again. There was Andrew, who just an hour before was humming along, doing fence repairs as a gift to his mom for Mother's Day. And now here was Andrew, facing surgery and the big question: would he have flexibility in that finger ever again? Suddenly, he was the one needing prayers.

He thought immediately of the God Box. For months now, he'd been reading other people's requests for prayer. Through them, he'd experienced how fragile life is, how important it is to trust, how powerful prayer is, and how good it is to be a part of a community. Sometimes he'd jot me a note to say he had just spent time staring at these requests on his computer screen while tears trickled down his face. Tears of compassion and gratitude for what he has, and tears of empathy. Life is fragile.

One of the first things Andrew thought of when the saw went through his finger was to get this powerful prayer network on its knees. He needed help. He trusted God would see him through this. He knew God as faithful. But there's nothing quite like having a cheering squad behind you to help focus God's attention right here, right now! And of course, there's nothing like having someone like myself who doesn't know one end of a saw from the other to do the reporting. I told everyone his finger had been run over by a chain saw. Table saw, chain saw, they're all the same, aren't they? No matter, I got the attention of the powerful prayer network, and the prayers began rising like incense for Andrew!

Days later, Andrew was back at the university, leaping over anything in his path with the balance and grace of a gazelle. "I, who have died, am alive again today, and this is the sun's birthday!"

5

Is the God Box Ever Full? Does Prayer Really Work?

One of the things I was reminded about right away when I started my online God Box was that no matter how much we put in it, it was never full! I used to begin a "busy" God Box week by saying that the Box was "full to the brim," until Carol from church corrected me, saying that God's Box is never full. She's right. No matter how many prayers we put before God, God is never overloaded or overwhelmed!

The movie *Bruce Almighty* shows us what might happen if the opposite were true. In a very funny and poignant scene, God (played by Morgan Freeman) hands over his divine power to Bruce Almighty (Jim Carrey). As Bruce gleefully—with that mischievous twinkle in his eye—assumes his godly nature, he begins to hear voices. He turns to God and asks, "What are all those voices?" God says, "Better pay attention to them or they'll build up on you." Bruce Almighty listens more carefully only to realize that millions upon millions of people are asking for everything under the sun. Voices in every language are buzzing in his ears at greater and greater speed and volume. He has quite literally become the God Box for the world!

Bruce scrambles to find a system to organize the prayers. He tries sorting them into file drawers, but that's too cumbersome. He tries Post-it notes, but there are so many of them that they become the wallpaper. Finally, he turns to his computer, and with fingers flying across the keyboard, he creates the Yahweh: You've Got Prayers Web site. The Hit counter for visitors to the site begins spinning to the thousands, millions, billions. The magnitude of world need becomes so overwhelming that Bruce is pushed right to the edge.

He decides to give everyone what they want. Standing proudly before his keyboard, with a most Carrey-like godly powerful move, he presses the Yes key. Then he waits for the voices to subside. Instantaneously, his magnanimous yes unleashes a torrent of chaos, anger, disorder, rage. Saying *yes* to everyone helps no one. *Yes* to everyone totally upsets the world order as one person's need flies in the face of another's.

Bruce sidles up to God Almighty and says, "I just gave them all they wanted." To which God replies, "Since when did anyone have a clue about what they wanted? Want to see a miracle, son? Be the miracle."

Thank God, God is God and Bruce is not! I like what the Morgan Freeman God says, though, about *being* the miracle. Rather than expecting to magically get everything we want with the flick of a computer key, God Almighty Freeman challenges Bruce, and us, to be the miracle. He invites participation.

Inspired by T. S. Eliot's *Four Quartets*, David Steindl-Rast says something similar: "Nothing will help us understand hope as much as a pilgrim's life, 'still and still moving,' day by day. And nothing will be more convincing to others as the way we exercise hope in our inner attitude and in our outward behavior."[14] Be the miracle. Be still and still moving.

In the stillness, we feel God's presence. The restlessness in us can rest; our thirsty soul is watered and refreshed. Remaining still, we gather courage; we know that God and others are with us. Still moving, we do everything we can to participate in the miracle. For me, with a cancer diagnosis, that meant eating right, exercising, praying, doing visualizations and affirmations, meditating, listening to good music, watching funny movies, laughing, playing, breathing, being with those I love, reconciling with those I find hard to love, soaking up natural wonders, petting my cat, letting my cat purr within me like God's own presence, accepting Reiki and Healing Touch, enjoying a good book, sitting in the sun, taking a nap, taking a bath (even at Lourdes), enjoying a massage, investigating cancer's causes and treatments, finding the needed resources, resting, laughing, praying, and sitting some more—being still, and still moving!

As we are still and still moving, we live into hope. Yet we know that no matter what we do, no matter how well we live, no matter how much we pray, things may not turn out the way we want. "Hope does not even pretend that everything will be all right," says Steindl-Rast. "Hope simply does its thing, like that spider in the corner of my bookshelf. She will make a new web again and again, as often as my feather duster swooshes it away—without self-pity, without self-congratulations, without expectations, without fear."[15] In the stillness, we know that everything depends on God, and then we keep moving, acting as if everything depends on us.

The intercessory prayer that fills up The God Box each week is an expression of hope. We hope that we will not have to "drink this cup" or that our friends might be spared the drinking. We would rather avoid the devastation of cancer or depression or brokenness or death itself. And so we cry out. We hope for something better. We pray for something better.

Our hopes become our prayer. *I hope I can complete this book, I hope that the fire will not come up the mountain. I hope that my relationships will be peaceful. I hope that the cancer doesn't come back. I hope that I'll make it to retirement, that the war will end, that the grass will grow, that the wine will flow, that my body stays fit, that my heart won't give out, that I'll always be happy, that I'll never give up, that my husband, Jerry, will live forever (at least until I die!). I hope everyone can have their most basic needs met, that there'll be an end to poverty and violence and destruction of all kinds. I hope, I hope, I hope, and every hope becomes a prayer. Please, God, please God, please God. Please don't let me suffer. Please don't let others suffer. Please don't let me go through pain or separation or loneliness or rejection or illness. Please just help me make it through. Keep me safe, O God.*

These are the prayers that fill up God's Box! This is the chatter that Bruce Almighty tried to stop with the one *great yes* to everything. But it doesn't work that way. Prayer is not magic. Even though we hope and pray that something magical will happen, we know from life experience that things don't always turn out the way we want.

I learned this when I was nine years old. I can remember praying every day, for a little baby brother or sister. I brought it up to God every day—morning, noon, and night. With great persistence, I begged God for a new baby brother or sister. My parents smiled lovingly and encouraged me to keep praying.

One day, my prayers were answered. My parents announced that in a few months, I was indeed going to have a little baby brother or sister. I jumped for joy, thanked God with all my heart and soul, and immediately began shopping for all the little pacifiers, bibs, and rattles my meager allowance would allow. Then one night, just weeks later, my mother got really sick. I can remember my friend Mimi's dad, the doctor, making a house call late that night. My mother had to go to the hospital right away. She was bleeding. She would have to stay overnight.

Little kids weren't allowed in hospital rooms in those days, but that didn't keep my brother and me away. The next day, we went to the hospital to visit. We waited outside, below my mother's room until, like the Pope, she appeared at her window and waved, showing us that everything was OK. We were relieved and excited to see her on her feet and were encouraged with the news that she'd be home in a day or so.

We weren't thinking about the new baby; it hadn't crossed our minds that our mother's sickness had anything to do with the baby. Our focus was on our mom. On the way home from the hospital, our attention shifted abruptly, however, as my dad stumbled over his words and his sadness to tell us that there would be no baby brother or sister. We didn't understand what had happened. What does a nine-year-old know about a miscarriage? My dad simply told us that having a new baby in the family just wasn't in God's plan at this time. I learned at that early age that it's OK to ask God for stuff, but I also learned that you don't always get what you want.

The nuns in grade school taught us that "the prayer of petition is the lowest form of prayer." That we should be focusing on the loftier prayers of adoration, thanks and praise, and forgiveness—not just these lowly "gimme prayers." It almost seemed like there was something unworthy or wrong about intercessory prayer. Yet Jesus himself used this kind of prayer in his most agonizing hour. *Father, let this cup pass.* If there was any chance he could avoid the crucifixion, he was open to it. He wasn't afraid to ask boldly. At the very crux of salvation itself, he let his preference be known. Perhaps our gimme prayers were redeemed in that moment. And yet there was something more. He continued, *Not my will but yours be done.* And with that, *we* were redeemed. The consequences of not getting what we ask for can be disappointing in one moment, yet surprising and promising in the next. We don't always get what we want, but God is always faithful.

David Steindl-Rast says that "all prayer is essentially an act of gratitude. Even the prayer of petition that boils up from some agonizing personal need includes, if it is authentic, a belief that 'God's will be done'—an expression of our utter dependence on God's mercy."[16] This dependence is where we end up when there is nowhere else to turn. It is the ultimate surrender: *I place my life into your hands.* It is where Anne Lamott landed when she was tired of driving the raggedy old bus of her concerns around and placed her need in her God Box. It is not a magic box. It is a symbol of surrender, a place to park our fears and longings, a place to park ourselves, trusting somehow that all will be well. It's the tent to which we retreat to experience being held in the embrace of God's strong arms, as well as the arms of those who love and care about us.

When I heard I might have cancer, my immediate response was to ask God to let this cup pass. I wasn't ready to die. I wasn't' ready to let go of the life I love. My professor's "oh no, not you" rattled in my head. Then I had this weird feeling that no matter what happened, it would be OK. *I* would be OK. *Thy will be done?* I didn't want to manipulate God's will. I wanted to *do* God's will—scary as it seemed in this moment. Drawing on trust that goes way back to my childhood, something rose in me that felt like courage. I relaxed even as tears rolled down my cheeks and as I wondered where all this would lead. I remembered that my God is a faithful God.

At the same time, a kind of ambivalence took hold of me that is somewhat difficult to describe. As I let go and decided that it really was in God's hands, that *I* was in God's hands, I also experienced a low-grade, almost subconscious fear that somehow I wasn't fighting hard enough. Had I surrendered without putting up a good fight? Fighting cancer, they say, takes everything you've got. If I didn't fight hard enough, would Jer end up a widower?

Bernie Siegel, cancer's "love doctor," says that "when you have accepted, retreated, and prepared yourself to fight, then you are ready to surrender. Again, you do not surrender to outcomes but to events. We waste so much energy fighting the nature of life. Accept the nature of life and surrender to it. When you do, you will have peace. When our energy is restored, we stop fighting things we cannot control, and we can start building our lives. Surrender is not about doing nothing; it is about doing the right things."[17] Being still and still moving.

Many studies have been conducted about the effect of prayer on healing. The big question is: "Does prayer work?" In a culture that reveres science and is skeptical about religion, there are plenty of scientific studies looking for proof. In his book, *Prayer Is Good Medicine*, bestselling author and physician, Larry Dossey, shares the results of some of these studies: "Prayer works," he says. "More than 130 controlled laboratory studies show, in general, that prayer or a prayer like state of compassion, empathy, and love can bring about healthful changes. Statistically speaking, prayer is effective."[18]

Sharon Fish Mooney, while critical of Larry Dossey's new age or new consciousness approach, agrees. She's found that "a growing number of studies in many disciplines, including sociology, medicine, and nursing, indicate that participation in religious practices of virtually all types correlates positively with health indicators, such as lower blood pressure, decreased depression and anxiety, and even lower mortality rates. Prayer is one of those practices."[19]

Larry Dossey goes on to say that "*Hope heals*. Faith helps mobilize a person's defenses and assists in getting well, and optimism leads generally to better outcomes. Hundreds of case histories and scientific studies affirm this observation."[20]

Michael McCullough, reviewed thirty-five of those scientific studies in 1995 and made four tentative conclusions about intercessory prayer: "First, prayer, especially prayer that is rich in mystical and religious experience, appears to be related to at least some measures of subjective well-being. Second, prayer is popularly relied upon for coping with difficult life circumstances and may serve a stress-deterrent effect during such circumstances. Third, the relationship between prayer and psychiatric symptoms remains unclear, although several investigations have yielded promising preliminary results. Fourth, though the empirical investigation of intercessory prayer has been plagued with methodological flaws, Byrd's (1988) well-designed study has pointed to how God heals through intercessory prayer."[21]

In April 2006, however, the results of a $2.4 million study (STEP – Study of Therapeutic Effects of Intercessory Prayer) put a bit of a damper on McCullough's optimistic conclusions and was a setback for those who believe in the power of prayer. Simply put, the study of 1,802 people who underwent coronary bypass surgery concluded that intercessory prayer doesn't help heart surgery patients. In fact, some fared worse when prayed for! Researchers are somewhat mystified by the results of the study, which raised as many questions as it answered and for which they have no clear explanations.[22]

While there has been much agreement among common everyday people and some researchers that "prayer works," there's still a fair amount of controversy surrounding the idea. And there's the deeper question: Should God be put to such scrutiny?

C. S. Lewis, one of the most influential Christian thinkers of the twentieth century, thinks it's ludicrous that we would even frame such a question "does prayer work?" For him, "The question then arises, 'What sort of evidence would prove the efficacy of prayer?' The thing we pray for may happen, but how can you ever know it was not going to happen anyway? Even if things were indisputably miraculous, it would not follow that the miracle had occurred because of your prayers. The answer surely is that a compulsive empirical proof such as we have in sciences can never be attained."[23]

What does your own lived experience tell you?

I have found myself saying out loud that "prayer works." I've heard other people say that I am a living example that "prayer works." But like C. S. Lewis, it makes me nervous to make such a bold proclamation. What if I had died? Would then our prayers not have "worked?" Would prayer have been "ineffective?"

I feel more comfortable talking about the *power* of prayer. By power, I mean energy and strength, not control. I know what it feels like to be buoyed up by the prayers of others. The very thought of people's prayerful intentions focused on me during chemotherapy strengthened my resolve to keep moving in the direction of health. The power of prayer is like the power of love and the power of gratitude. It does something to you. It transforms you. It keeps you moving.

On the Sunday before my surgery, I went to Mass at UCSD. After communion, after singing, "Eat this bread, drink this cup, come to me and never be hungry," through tears, I stood in the center aisle of the church for the Sacrament of the Sick, which includes anointing with oil and the laying on of hands. I had participated in this ritual so many times before, but never as the one to be anointed. So many feelings were pulsing through me as I stood there with everyone turned toward me, their hands either touching me or touching someone else who was touching me. I felt a little awkward, humbled indeed, hopeful yet tentative, open to grace. Above all, I felt love and gratitude. I was immersed in it. I was floating on it.

As the community laid its hands on me, I experienced the peace, the calm, the strength, the courage, the power of all those hands on me. I experienced love in those hands. The faith in the room was palpable. The love, tangible. Time was suspended. Fear of tomorrow gave way to the power of now. As the holy oil of the sick oozed down my forehead, calmness swept over me. I was not alone.

I could never know what God's will for me was in that moment. I did not know if I would live or die. But I knew that I was surrounded by possibility as I laid myself open to love and healing and grace. I was filled with hope, with what William Sloane Coffin calls a "passion for the possible." My mind, body, and spirit were in sync. The more I let go, the more I relaxed in love's embrace and experienced God's healing touch.

Larry Dossey says that "experiments in prayer suggest that love is one of the most important factors influencing its effectiveness."[24] Love was in those hands laid on me in church, but it also came knocking at my door. People and flowers and food and quilts and books showed up in abundance. As people remembered me in prayer, they were reminded to remember me in person. Live or die, all of these experiences of loving prayer and the actions that flowed from them were life-giving. All of these prayerful gestures—my own and those of others—were powerful healing gestures and clues to how prayer "works." Trustworthy friends mirrored a trustworthy God. Placing my life in God's hands seemed easy.

Corita Kent, the young nun whose serigraphs hung in office buildings in the '60s once proclaimed in big bold letters and colors that "to believe in God is to know that all the rules will be fair and there will be wonderful surprises" and that "God writes straight with crooked lines." Those two lines say a lot to me about having a passion for possibility as well as a penchant for accepting God's will.

The Scriptures are filled with passion for the possible. Just look at it rippling through these lines from both the Hebrew and the Christian Scriptures:

> The Lord hears when I call out. (Ps 4:4)

> Believe that you will receive it and it shall be yours. (Mk 11:24)

> For God, all things are possible. (Mt 19:26)

> Ask and you will receive . . . everyone who asks, receives. (Lk 11:9–10)

The fervent prayer of a righteous person is very powerful. (Jas 5:16)

Have no anxiety at all . . . by prayer and petition, with thanksgiving, make your requests known to God. (Phil 4:6)

Whatever you ask in my name, I will do . . . if you ask anything in my name, I will do it. (Jn 14:13–14)

So we fasted, and prayed to our God for this, and our petition was granted. (Ezr 8:23)

These are the mantras for midnight that people of faith hang on to in times of trouble. These are the words that bolster our courage and help us trust. Having heard them often, they spring to mind easily; remembering them relieves fears. The miracle stories in the Gospels do the same thing. When we hear the story of the crippled man picking up his pallet and walking or the hemorrhaging woman touching the hem of Jesus's garment with great faith and then being healed, we see that healing is possible. What happened to them could happen to us. Faith moves mountains, doesn't it? These stories stimulate a passion for the possible and open us to God's surprises. They give us hope. This is a good thing, yet every one of these passages has to be seen against the backdrop of Gethsemane. *Not my will but yours be done.* Redemption from suffering comes when we surrender. Redemption from suffering comes when we "let go and let God." The Scriptures encourage us to be bold, to do what Jesus did: Ask. Then, surrender. Sometimes, as we surrender, we get more than we could ever have bargained for, as Jesus did, and as did the anonymous confederate soldier to whom this poem is attributed:

I asked God for strength that I might achieve;
I was made weak that I might learn to obey.

I asked for health that I might do great things;
I was given infirmity, that I might do better things.

I asked for riches that I might be happy;
I was given poverty that I might be wise.

I asked for power that I might have the praise of men;
I was given weakness, that I might feel the need of God.

I asked for all things that I might enjoy life;
I was given life that I might enjoy all things.

I got nothing that I had asked for,
But everything I had hoped for.

Almost despite myself my unspoken prayers were answered;
I am, among all men, most richly blessed.

Does prayer work? My experience says "yes!" I have found that as I pray and as others pray with me, something happens to *me*. I am not the same. I am less afraid, more trusting; less anxious, more positive; less concerned about tomorrow, more interested in today. I find relief. I relax. I breathe easier. I experience hope. I keep moving. Prayer works in all these miraculous ways. I don't need to control the results; nor do I need to be controlled by circumstances. I trust that in God, all will be well. That, to me, is powerful. That, to me, is the way "prayer works."

What do you think? Does prayer work? The God Box Community responds.

- ❖ It was such a comfort to know that God Box prayers were being said for my recovery throughout my six months of cancer treatment. I felt such positive strength that I know was from all the prayers that were being said for me.

- ❖ This collection of inspiration and reflection reminds me to never underestimate the power of love and empathy when people are taking on the fight of (and for) their life.

- ❖ The God box only adds to one's belief and faith in the power of prayer. God never let's us down especially when one or more gather in prayer and even more so when all are praying for common concerns. As our pastor stated a few Sundays ago, God wants us to be bold in our prayers.

- ❖ I do believe strongly in the power of prayer and that God answers those prayers—often in mysterious ways. Ways that we could never think of and sometimes don't understand.

- ❖ I have a question, and I am sure you share it. What do people think is happening when they pray the prayer of intercession? What is their "theology" of this kind of prayer? And does this kind of prayer tend to keep some people in an immature, even magical dependence on and relationship with God?

- ❖ From time to time, the vastness of needs prompts me to think how busy heaven must be with all of the God's family launching these concerns throughout our days. What a marvelous reminder of the communion of saints!

❖ It is wonderful that as a community, we can pray together and use our "prayer strength" to support those who at difficult times may not have the "strength" to pray.

❖ I have been so impressed with the God Box and its writings. As a twenty-three-year psychotherapist, I have found that the medical model is not totally adequate for healing. Much of our need as human beings requires an integration of the psychological, emotional, and spiritual. I plan to use this book with my patients, young and old, as a resource that is most valuable and will provide a new support structure.

❖ We find those prayer requests we make are often answered, not necessarily the way we thought God should respond, but he responded and we feel the outcome is always more positive with his participation!

Prayer at its best requires from many of us that we give up all naïve notions of God, emptying ourselves of all intention and manipulation, all expectations and demands and exposing ourselves to absolute affectionate emptiness . . . Prayer acknowledges fear and takes us beyond it. What could be more elegant?

—Thomas Moore

You do what you can. Then you get out of the way, because you're not the one who does the work.

—Anne Lamott

Wherever I turn, you are there.

—Nicholas of Cusa

6

Were We Wrong to Pray for a Miracle?

That's the question that weighed heavily on everyone's mind as we filed by Kathy's casket to pay our last respects. We had watched myelofibrosis ravage her body for five years, taking first her strength, then her spleen, then an eye, and too often her energy to simply be the mother she wanted to be to her three lovely daughters. Kathy was an optimistic fighter who focused, even with just one eye, on the positives that could be found in her dire situation. But the disease was winning.

On the final night of Kathy's battle for life, we were summoned to her bedside. Summoned to gather her children, splashing in a nearby hotel pool, having a taste of the summer their parents were determined they would not miss. Summoned to answer the youngest's question: "Is my mom going to die?"

When we arrived at the hospital, Kathy was no longer breathing on her own. A noisy machine picked up the pace for her and signaled an ever more dire situation. We kept vigil, praying through the night as the respirator pumped in and out, in and out, rhythmically, noisily, laboriously. Richard stood over his wife's lifeless, mechanically breathing body and continued praying for a miracle.

In the tiny visitor-waiting room, the rest of us huddled together and prayed the rosary in low, somber tones throughout the night, holding on to God and each other—and held by grace. Never did this rosary of my childhood practice have such an impact on me. Never had I appreciated so much having at my fingertips those beads, with familiar words and a familiar cadence. Never had I experienced the Communion of Saints so forcefully. Familiar Holy Week litanies played in my head. Hailing Mary was never more earnest or more faith-filled. Never had Mary come to my aid so tangibly than in that moment. Mary was with us. God was with us. Huddled together in this foxhole of our lives, we were one in our desire and in our faith that all will be well.

Richard continued to hope and pray for the miracle to happen.

The next afternoon, Kathy died.

At the funeral, Fr. Paul did not dodge the question. "Were we wrong to pray for a miracle?" he asked. I squirmed in my seat. We had been praying for a miracle forever, it seemed and Richard had his heart set on it. His faith was strong. He believed that faith could move mountains. He had engaged a whole community in praying Kathy back to health. Was he wrong to do so? Were we all wrong to hope and pray for a miracle? Fr. Paul might just as well have asked: Were we trying to manipulate God's will?

Then, Father Paul unstrung the bow. "No, we were not wrong to pray for a miracle. Look around this church," he said. "Look at how many people are here." The pews were packed, and a line had circled around the church for hours before the funeral—hundreds of friends waiting to pass by Kathy one last time to bid farewell. "Look around and see all the people here who have supported this family day after day for five long years. Look at those who delivered meals and love every day for weeks, for months, for all five years of Kathy's illness. Look at those who helped with transportation, cleaning, errands; those who gave their evenings to be with the children while Richard visited Kathy at the hospital. Look at those who walked with Richard, prayed with him, listened to him. Those who helped Kathy check things off her lists . . . cards to get, books to return, kids to encourage. The miracle we got may not have been the one we were praying for, but just look around you and see the miracle that did happen. This community has never been more alive, nor has it reached out more effectively. When called upon for its support, this community showed up! Wonder of wonders . . . God's miracle wasn't the one we were praying for, but it is certainly one we delight in."

We don't always get what we pray for, but God is ever faithful. We witness this so often in the God Box. I can remember praying for Jean's friend who was dying. Hand-wringing family and friends watched as the cancer relentlessly devoured their friend, their daughter. An update came; things didn't look good. In fact, the situation was deteriorating. Then one day, the news came that Lianne had died. And when she did, Jean asked me to put a note in the "praise and thanks" column of the God Box. She wanted everyone to know that Lianne died peacefully. "It was a long day," Jean said, "but frankly one I was sad to see end because of the wonderful miracles God was providing each of us for the closure we needed." There was so much peace to soak up in that room that it was difficult to walk away. Their hearts were filled with deep love and abiding peace. They would never be the same.

What happens to *us* as we pray is just as important as what happens or doesn't happen for those for whom we pray. It's a lot like working for justice. We can march in demonstration after demonstration, trying to change the will of the people to move from war to peace, from privilege and disproportionate wealth to economic well-being for all — feeling like we are getting nowhere. I remember hearing a political activist once say that he was often asked, "Why do you do those things? Why do you protest, write letters, vote? Things never change." His response? "No, things don't often change the way I'd like them to, but I do. I become kinder, gentler, more patient, more tolerant, more loving."

Prayer works like that. We don't always get what we want, but we become more aligned, more peaceful with God's design. We may struggle to accept God's will, but on a deeper level, we can "be still and know that I am God."

Who me? Believe in miracles? The Community responds.

❖ I have always believed in the power of prayer. But after seeing what small and large miracles-group prayer has accomplished, it has further strengthened my faith and belief in prayer.

❖ It has helped me pray more gratefully, of course. But it has also given me the courage to pray for miracles more directly.

❖ Just an update on my colleague who had metastatic cancer who was prayed for in the God Box last year. I must say that I was not optimistic about her prognosis with her tumor. But the tumor has regressed significantly (beaten back by prayer, surgery, and chemotherapy), and she plans to be back at work. This seems miraculous to me.

❖ I love coming together like this in prayer. I've seen miracles happen in my own life but find it even more inspiring to read about miracles happening every day because we are all praying.

Prayer is not asking for what you think you want, but asking to be changed in ways you can't imagine.

—Kathleen Norris

Modern scholars talk about prayer as performance language. It doesn't merely express. It accomplishes something, and one of the things it accomplishes is holiness.

—Thomas Moore

7

Standing in the Need of Prayer

I let the cat out of the bag immediately. I told everyone I know that I might have cancer. It occurred to me that I should wait—wait until I knew whether or not I really had cancer—whether or not I really needed their prayers. Then it dawned on me. What if their prayers could work the miracle you sometimes hear about? You know the one where the doctor goes inside and, much to her amazement, finds nothing? Where cancer was suspected, there is none? What if their prayers could relieve my fear? Or help me accept my situation? What if their prayers could help Jerry cope? I decided not to delay. I knew my friends would jump on board, get on their knees, or send up smoke signals with incense or candles to ask God's protection, God's favor, God's tender loving presence to be with me.

When the doctor's voice dropped as she revealed numbers that were far beyond the norm, when she told me an *oncologist* would be involved in what was supposed to be a routine hysterectomy, when an appointment was made for me at the Women's *Cancer* Center, I got scared. I was beyond scared; I was numb.

Where do you go with that kind of information? I suppose I could have gone into depression or panic or rage. I chose to go to my friends—fast as I could. And I asked them to pray. Something inside of me said that prayer helps, that the more people praying, the better.

I'm someone who grew up on prayer. We prayed in the car on summer driving vacations. We prayed before meals, and after them, too. We prayed the rosary around my parents' bed each night. We spent all of Holy Week in church, working our way toward Easter. There were Tuesday night Mother of Perpetual Help devotions, First Friday benedictions, novenas in Mary's month of May. We prayed before each class in our Catholic grade school and before every Girl Scout meeting after school. In my convent days, I learned to pray the Liturgy of the Hours and how to pray with Scripture. As life went on, I learned how to meditate, contemplate, center myself. I guess you could say that my whole life was a training ground for learning how to pray and a practice ground for doing it.

I can remember speaking to students at our Welcome Mass at UCSD after my first round of chemotherapy. I told them that I had cancer and that I was counting on their prayers. There's something about young people's prayers that seems most efficacious to me. Knowing that the students were praying for me gave me the greatest solace of all. Young, vibrant hearts in touch with a compassionate, tender God, asking on my behalf— what could be sweeter than that?

I encouraged the students that day not only to pray for me but to develop their own prayer lives while they were in college—to practice now so the resource would be there when they needed it. I used Steven Covey's "Law of the Farm" to make my point. If a farmer wants a rich harvest, he needs to prepare the soil, nurture it, fertilize it, water it, weed it. Just as a farmer can't grow a good crop overnight, I told them, you can't grow your faith overnight.

The next day at the oncologist's office, I reported "what I was able to do over the weekend." I told my doctor about my talk at Welcome Mass and how I had encouraged the students to develop their faith life day by day while they were in college—to practice for the big events of life. My point seemed lost on the doctor. He countered with the experience of an oncologist. "There are no atheists in cancer wards," he said. Cancer patients leap into God's lap pretty quickly, pretty easily, whether they prayed every day of their life or not at all.

OK, that's true. There are no atheists in foxholes. And while it's true that God is always there waiting for us, ready to hold us in loving arms, no matter how much attention we've paid, it's also true that our sense of intimacy and trust rely on some level of familiarity. "It's the time you waste on your rose that makes your rose so important," says the Little Prince. Likewise, it's the time you waste on your relationships that make them so important. And it's the time you waste with God that makes God so important, so accessible, such a source of comfort. Words come more easily when you've said them often. Trust comes easier when you've experienced trust before. It's the time you waste on prayer that gives you the words to say, hope to hang on to, trust to get you through.

As I lay in bed waiting for surgery, and recovery from surgery, I found myself praying easily, asking boldly, trusting widely through tears, of course.

I had a whole list of saints to invoke—cherished travel partners who were somehow in this with me. *"Mother Mary, pray for me. St. Catherine of Siena, pray for me. Dorothy Day, pray for me. Hildegard of Bingen, pray for me. All you holy men and women, pray for me."*

I had words to say, words I'd memorized in my youth. From the traditional Memorare: *"Remember O most gracious Virgin Mary that never was it known that anyone who fled to thy protection, implored thy help or sought thy intercession was left unaided . . ."*

And from the Magnificat: *"For The One who is mighty has done great things for me. Holy is God's name."*

I knew how to breathe so that God's breath would breathe through me, release my anxiety, untie my knots.

I knew how to let go of thoughts, let go of words and simply sit, centered in God's love.

One-liners I'd collected over the years came to my rescue in the lonely darkness of the night: *"All will be well. All will be well,"* and *"Be with me, Lord, when I am in sorrow and pain."*

Familiar hymns played in my head:

Amazing grace, how sweet the sound that saved someone like me . . .

Take O take me as I am; summon out what I shall be . . .

Eat this bread, drink this cup, come to me and never be hungry . . .
Eat this bread, drink this cup, trust in me and you'll never thirst . . .

The Psalms were there for me:
The Lord is my shepherd, there is nothing I lack . . . Even when I walk through a dark valley, I fear no harm for you are at my side. (23)

The Lord is my light and my salvation, whom do I fear? (27)

Newer translations for *praying* the Psalms refreshed old images and became my favorites:

For I shall hide in Love's heart in the days of trouble,
As in a tent in the desert,
Away from the noise of my fears . . .
Enfold me in your strong arms,
O Blessed One. (27)

Images from Scripture gave me reason to hope:

The hemorrhaging woman stopped bleeding.
Lazarus was raised from the dead.

Yes, God is always there waiting for us with open arms, but the more we do our part to develop our relationship, the more time we waste on it throughout life, the more we have to draw from in those "moments when . . ."

I am grateful to have so many resources at my fingertips. I'm also lucky not to have to pray for myself all by myself. When everyone started praying for me, I felt like I could relax a bit. I didn't have to carry the burden alone anymore.

Others were helping me. Others kept my intention alive as I rested and took care of myself. There was a tremendous sense of relief in that.

When I was a kid, there were candles in every church — real candles. They were called vigil or votive lights. We'd light them for a special intention and then pray for that intention for a few minutes while we watched the candle burn. When we left the church, we were told that the candle would keep burning and would symbolically continue our prayer for us while we went about our business.

When everyone started praying for me, I felt as if vigil lights had been lit all over the world. I could go about the business of getting well while all the prayers continued. It provided such a sense of well-being. I felt loved, cherished, cared for, held. I relaxed, knowing I wasn't in this all by myself. Standing in the need of prayer, I was never left unaided.

What's your experience of prayer and the God Box? The Community responds.

❖ I get teary when I think of all the support that's come my way. The best part is how simple, natural, and "of-course" it is to pass it on.

❖ My journey this Easter is one I will never forget. On Ash Wednesday, I was put in the hospital for emergency surgery on my brain; they found a cyst. Right away I called my friend and asked her to put me in the God Box. After that I stopped worrying because I knew with all my heart that my prayers were going to be answered. To know that so many people that you don't even know are praying for you gives you such comfort . . . you can't buy medicine like that.

❖ I always have believed in the power of prayer. Knowing that there are so many people out there praying for each other is a very comforting feeling.

❖ I find it helps people when they are in a stressful situation to know that you can do this for them. They seem genuinely relieved. The prayer in the God Box is like compounded interest . . . it adds up!

❖ For our family, extended family, friends, friends of friends, etc . . . we have experienced the profound healing power of prayer through Fiona's ordeal and hope to share that with whoever needs a prayer.

❖ The *God Box* has kept from me the delusion that most people most of the time aren't in the need of prayer, don't have life-threatening challenges or insoluble problems to face.

❖ I am not a particularly "prayerful" person, so while I take time to read the God Box, I don't find myself saying any separate prayers because of it. I am moved by the confidence that people can place in prayer although I do not personally feel that confidence.

❖ I know that if I need some prayers for something, I have a whole community out there who is willing to help me pray.

❖ Just today I was pruning my apple tree in the backyard with Bee. Of course I was up too high on the ladder and the ground is muddy, I started to tip over but righted myself before I became an entry on your God Box. I was actually thinking what it would read: "And for Frank who is in the hospital after falling over on a ladder in his backyard, pray for his broken back to mend," something like that. So I think of it more than even I know, and my experience of it has been one of thankfulness and sorrow at the same time. I am thankful because I read about how bad off some have it and sorry because it takes this for me to realize at times, that I have been blessed in abundance by our loving Lord. So for me, it is a humbling experience to say the least.

❖ My experience is one of awe. I read the email and feel humbled by the sufferings of others . . . theirs without complaint, just faith in God and hope of God hearing all who are speaking, begging, and asking in their name.

❖ I've been prayed for and felt the strength of the prayers during my cancer surgery and treatment. It was very peaceful knowing so many people were praying for me; I found an inner strength and sense of calm.

❖ I've got to tell you that I still get choked up when I begin to pray for the needs in the God Box.

It's me, it's me, it's me, O Lord, standing in the need of prayer.
—Traditional Black Gospel Song, Author unknown

8

Seeing What Others Do

Prayer intentions in the God Box are released each week like doves, carrying the hopes and fears of those in need to friends and strangers who have promised to pray. If you've ever seen doves released into the sky at a wedding to celebrate the bride and groom's love-taking flight or at a funeral to let a loved one go, you've heard that hushed "ah" that rises up with the doves and the silence that follows as they disappear high into the sky. It's a little like that each week as I release the intentions in the God Box. Names of individuals and groups show up briefly on my computer screen, then with the stroke of a key, the intentions take flight across the globe and will reach their destination within seconds.

And at that moment, that old saying crosses my mind: "I know what I am giving them; I do not know what they will receive." I do not know if my email will come as a gift, a challenge, an annoyance, a sobering reality, an opportunity to be grateful, or something else.

And so it was music to my ears when Suzanne said to me, with a smile from ear to ear, how much she loved receiving the God Box. She told me how grateful she was for this opportunity to *be there* for others and how humbled she felt regarding her own good fortune in life. I could see that she was actually honored to be able to offer compassion and love to the people in the God Box, most of whom she's never met.

That was striking enough, but she went on. She began to tell me what she does with the intentions each week. She prints out the abbreviated list of names "in a nutshell" that I include at the end of the God Box and takes it with her to the beach every day when she goes for her hour-long walk at lunchtime. As she walks, she prays. And as she prays, she remembers each person on the list and asks God's blessings on them. She spends time with them on a beach far away — people she doesn't even know, mixed in with a few she does. She sings little chants or verses to herself as she remembers them. As Suzanne described her daily practice, I imagined her energy being released across the planet, just like those little doves; and I felt confident that somewhere, somehow, someone was experiencing relief as Suzanne prayed.

I was so impressed and inspired by Suzanne's daily routine that I told everyone in the God Box about it the following week. I asked if there were any other innovations out there. My friend G wrote back:

> Praying? My praying runs in curious loops and cycles.
>
> I have literally had my own little altar with its tin box of Mexican milagros[25] for some twelve years now. It stands open next to my Black Madonna. She, in turn, stands on a blue tapestry. For a long time, I simply drew a simple picture of the person I was praying for and slipped it under the mat and put my hands over this as I thought about them. Those were times when I thought I didn't have any words left in me to bring before heaven. But then there are the cycles when the psalms come back or the prayers of Lauds and Compline work wonders again and bring comfort just for the oldness of their words.
>
> Sometimes I don't know how the person looks for whom I am praying, so I cannot draw them. Then I just pray for them. But each day I dip into my box of milagros and pull up an object and think about what this could mean for all these people and for this day: a pair of eyes. A leg. A heart. Breasts. A small boy. A woman . . . This object I put at the Virgin's feet for the day and give it to her care while I go about my day, pondering all the implications of what I drew from that box as the day began.

And when I need to do something totally different, I have a stash of candles to help with prayer. I always think that when I go off for the day or go to sleep at the end of the day, the candle will continue my prayer for me. Its flame licks and flickers with an energy and pleading of its own. It gives up its pillar of wax in an offering of flame and prayer. Do I dare to leave a candle burning when I leave the house?

Well, only if I set it either in the bathtub or now that I have one, in the fireplace. I have friends throughout the Midwest who have joined me in what we call our "bathtub prayers."

Mentioning G's bathtub prayers in the God Box encouraged another Midwesterner to send in a variation on the theme. Her friend keeps a candle burning night and day for her son fighting the war in Iraq. But when she leaves home or goes to sleep, she places her lit candle safely in the kitchen sink!

From beach prayers to bathtub and kitchen-sink prayers, we see what others do and are inspired. The God Box has become a playground for innovative prayer. Not only are participants finding new ways to pray, they are praying more often and in more places. Many are surprised to find themselves praying at their computer, sometimes several times a day. It had never crossed their mind that cyberspace could become sacred space. While they are multitasking their way through the day, sorting through phone messages, emails, and important papers and projects at their desk, the God Box arrives and it stops them in their tracks. As they read through the list of intentions, they see someone else taking on the fight of their life. They feel lucky, spared, grateful, full of compassion. Some sit right there in front of their computer in silence for a few minutes, asking God to help those on the list. Then they whisper a word of gratitude for their own good health this day. Suddenly, they no longer *have* to work; they are *able* to work.

Young mothers have discovered the sacredness of cyberspace. My cousin Bee tells me: "I made my own 'internet chapel,' lit a candle by the monitor, and prayed for my God Box friends right at the computer; it was quiet (all kids had left for school) and peace-filled. I will try that again another day!"

Monica, another young mother, chimes in: "I pray at the computer by the kitchen anytime I get a chance. I pray as I am reading the email . . . I use the email as a meditation tool! Since I don't get a chance to pray by myself anywhere else with the busyness of taking care of the house and the kids, this has had a huge effect on my prayer life. It has modernized the way I pray. I never thought I would find prayer in a computer. The fact that it is in my email and that I read it in silence . . . is wonderful!"

The God Box has become a vehicle for family and bedtime prayers with children as well. Emily tells me. "The God Box has helped us learn to pray as a family . . . with input from everyone. What a blessing to hear exactly who Fiona and Moira have been thinking about and why they want to add that particular person to the God Box! Before, we simply said a 'Bless us, O Lord' followed by either Brian or myself asking for prayers for those who we knew needed them and prayers of thanksgiving. Now that the kids are older, the God Box has allowed them to have a voice in our nightly prayer, too! Moira and Fiona like to write down the names of those we're praying for and put those pieces of paper in our 'God Box' next to the dining room table for nightly dinner prayer. The girls decorated a small box, and we put small strips of paper and a pen next to it . . . all on a tray near the table."

Pam says that "when little David and I pray together at night before bed, we always ask God to especially bless all the people in 'Miss Lynn's God Box.' I have not shared specific names, illnesses, or accidents with David, but we pray for all those in your God Box overall."

Personally, I like to print out the list and keep a votive candle burning on top of my stack of God Box emails as I work. Each time my eyes catch sight of the candle, I am reminded again to let my prayer rise up. I become mindful again and again of those in need and praise God for my own health this day. I'd have to say that lighting candles—while I'm working at my desk, while I'm cooking, while I'm praying, even while I'm bathing—has become my favorite way of keeping God Box intentions alive throughout the week.

My friend David figured out how to create our very own "God Box" Candle page at www.gratefulness.org, so now candles can burn in cyberspace for those in the

God Box. For my Catholic friend Ginny, this has become a very special experience. She says it puts her down on her knees in prayer, in front of the bank of candles of her childhood. Her Presbyterian husband is intrigued to try this practice!

Mindfulness is heightened as participants read each week's God Box. They find themselves praying in places and spaces they hadn't thought of before. Some print the names, cut out the names, contain the names, or even forget the names. Some walk with the names, drive with the names, talk with the names, or sit with the names. Some finger beads, pray formal prayers, or say nothing. Some practice centering prayer or meditation, some send Reiki to those willing to accept it, some sit with the Sacred Presence in adoration.

We all suffer, and somehow, as we are exposed to the suffering of others, our own responsiveness is ignited. We know that life is fragile as we watch others confront major illnesses and life challenges that seem to come out of nowhere. We know that we are not exempt. Seeing what others do, we are renewed in our own practice of praying for one another. We open the Box for yet another week. We open ourselves yet again to the heavy burden it carries. And then we get busy!

What do you do when **the** *God Box arrives?* *The Community responds.*

> ❖ I begin praying immediately for the people on the list. I try to take time periodically throughout my day. I do not remember all the names . . . but I know God knows when I say "the list!"
>
> ❖ I can't tell you how many times during the week when The God Box needs come to mind—in a variety of places: exercising, at Mass, before retiring, during reflective moments, etc.

❖ I pray at the computer; and sometimes a few of the requests I write on a small piece of paper, and they land in my box. Some requests come to mind during the day, and then I "hold these persons in the light"—usually for a very short time, but often more than once or twice, during the day. Every two or three weeks, I sit down at a table with my box. I light a candle and proceed to unfold one petition after another. I'm "reviewing," or making an "inventory" of what my box holds. I don't want it to gather moss . . . This action refreshes my heart and mind and makes me realize that I should pray more and/or more often. Whenever I come across a petition, which has been answered, I place that piece of paper with a big thank you into a small white box made of cardboard. Thus space is made in the main box for new petitions. And the other slips of paper with their various prayer requests are prayed for again while being refolded and placed back into the big box.

❖ I pray every Tuesday night with a group of fifteen to twenty-five people. It is a contemplative prayer group, so our prayer is in silence. But we have a strong belief that when we sit down, we bring all the needs of the world, including the specific needs of anyone who has asked for our prayers, into the silence—into the divine presence where these needs can be touched and met with God's mercy and love. Sometimes I print your page of weekly intentions and fold it on our little prayer altar as a symbol of our intention to pray for you and all those you love. We strongly believe in the communion of all those who seek God in prayer and in the mystical body that we form when we join together in prayer. All things are possible through Christ who strengthens us!

❖ I am more attentive to "catching the little moments" throughout the day to say some short prayers. I pray more "globally" so to speak, for all those who've requested his grace (mostly because I can't remember names so well)! I also think that just reading the requests with a prayerful heart is a prayer to God. My heart is often heavy for all those suffering.

❖ I usually save them to a folder and sometimes print them to cut out the list and add it to our little wooden God Box on our dining room table. I really love the addition of a prayer or thought that you do at the end. I hope to read some of these books/authors one of these days.

❖ Here is my daily prayer routine (adapted from Unity). I walk for an hour each day at the beach and as I walk I pray.

  • Part I: Petition. I mention my personal intentions and the needs of the people in the God Box.

  • Part 2: Thanksgiving. Thank God for all his blessings.

  • Part 3: Affirmation. I sometimes use the one from *The Daily Word*, but more frequently I use the daily Prayer for Peace. I repeat each line many times as I meditate. And all this takes up the hour. If I finish the prayer earlier, I will sometimes sing (in my head) one of the songs we've been singing in church. "Lead me, guide me. It's me, it's me, O Lord." One that I used a lot during the Lenten Season was "I Place My Life Into Your Hands."

❖ At the end of the General Intercessions at Mass on Sunday, we often have the "and for all the silent prayers in your hearts" pause at the end followed by "Lord, hear our prayer." I always pray for all the intentions of the God Box. Even though I cannot remember them all off the top of my head, I know God can remember them and understands my prayers better than I do.

❖ The God Box has become a family SOP (Standard Operating Procedure) to pray for all those in the God Box during our evening blessing before dinner.

❖ Besides praying with our family, we do ask for special intentions during our monthly married couples' dinner (a group of six to seven couples) at our church.

❖ I take time at work when the God Box comes to pray for those in need of our prayers and to reflect on the many graces the Lord gives us.

❖ I pray for the people in the God Box every morning on the way to school at the stoplights.

❖ I do read the God Box every week and pray for each of the listees. I click a "save" button so that I keep the God Box in my "Inbox" for the week until the new one arrives to replace it. And from time to time, I reread the list and the needs and pray.

❖ Bee and I pray for those in the God Box often at mealtimes but more consistently at adoration twice a week for one hour.

❖ As with most things in my life, the really important things happen between my commitments—in the car, as I wait for Mass to start, right before I go to sleep, sitting at the computer, at the prayer before meals. In those odd moments of the day, when my mind is free to wonder, I often talk to God.

❖ I pray for those in the God Box in the late evening. I print out the "list in a nutshell." I put the people at God's feet and leave them and myself there. He knows the need. Sometimes I find myself remembering them in the morning and praying for them. I am not a morning person, so I wait for as long as I can to turn off the alarm clock. My morning prayer is during my shower! God is not picky. For myself to pray, I need to quiet myself (my brain) down and have a short but quality time with the Lord. And many times when his presence is stronger, I pray, meditate, or just be there, for well over one and a half hour. That is a gift from him. It is at these times (even the short ones) that I bring the names on the list and ask him to hold them in his hands. Praying in that way for people I do not even know has helped me to be more aware of our oneness with each other and God. These evening prayers bring peace, hope, and warmth to me.

❖ I have asked dear friends and my eighty-three-year-old mother, a great prayer, to pray for intentions which particularly move me.

❖ The God Box has called me to weekly prayer outside my own routine! I have used it in family prayer but generally use it in my own quiet time that I have created in opening the box at the email site. I include a short prayer before opening it, calling on my own mindset to be open, to hear the calling, to request intercession from my angels/saints to those who are in need.

❖ Every morning I do my yoga then a special meditation/prayer. It is at this time that I include all of the names in the God Box.

❖ I always pray going up and down any stairs. Very often, I pray as I am driving. Music is my soul, so when I listen to music and turn my soul to the Lord, I remember all in the God Box and the one who originated it. How could I not involve others? I will run off the prayer sheet(s) and place one in chapel and one on the mail table. This reminds all of us that people depend on us to intercede for their needs. Whenever opportunity lends itself, I involve people with whom I am speaking, meetings which I attend, and when I am a presenter asking for all to remember all friends' needs in our God Box. Today's list already has been lifted once to the Lord and will be many more times from our refrigerator to bedroom doors, to our community at large, and to our small community. I extend the wish for prayers to Germany; as today we have company here from Germany.

To light a candle by myself is one of my favorite prayers. I am not talking about reading prayers by candlelight. The very act of lighting the candle is prayer. There is the sound of striking the match, the whiff of smoke after blowing it out, the way the flame flares up and then sinks, almost goes out until a drop of melted wax gives it strength to grow to its proper size and to steady itself. All this and the darkness beyond my small circle of light is prayer. I enter it as one enters a room.

—David Steindl-Rast, *Gratefulness, the Heart of Prayer*, 57.

It is not what we do that makes us holy. We make holy what we do.

—Meister Eckhart

I've recently rediscovered the rosary as a prayer form I haven't used in many years. In this stage of my life, I find it powerful. I just let the beads go through my fingers and say the phrases over and over again, and for some reason it stops the racing of my mind. It allows me to live in the center, in the present—not in the past or the future. After I started praying the rosary, all sorts of things fell into place, and my dream of The Center for

Action and Contemplation became a reality. I am not trying to say there's a magical way to get God to do what you want to do. That would be a misunderstanding of the power of prayer. But I do know the rosary was a prayer form given to me to help get myself out of the way. With the rosary, I could listen. I could surrender and trust so I could become some sort of instrument, as Francis would have said, some kind of channel of whatever it was that God wanted to do. And I think that's the purpose of all our prayer; not to prove ourselves to God or to bend the arm of God, but quite simply, to be able to listen anew.

—Richard Rohr, *Spirituality of Subtraction*

Many and Varied Ways to Pray

Prayer Flags: The color of a prayer flag and the symbols printed on it create a prayer of offering that the wind distributes to the world each time it brushes against the flag. The Tibetan word for a horizontal prayer flag is *Lung ta,* which translates literally as "wind horse." The prayers of a flag become a permanent part of the universe as the images fade from wind and sun. Just as life moves on and is replaced by new life, Tibetans renew their hopes for the world by continually mounting new flags alongside the old.

Tibetan Prayer Wheels (called *Mani* wheels by the Tibetans) are devices for spreading spiritual blessings and well-being. Rolls of thin paper, imprinted with many, many copies of the mantra (prayer) *Om Mani Padme Hum,* printed in an ancient Indian script or in Tibetan script, are wound around an axle in a protective container, and spun around and around. Typically, larger decorative versions of the syllables of the mantra are also carved on the outside cover of the wheel. Tibetan Buddhists believe that saying this mantra out loud or silently to oneself invokes the powerful benevolent attention and blessings of Chenrezig, the embodiment of compassion.

Like a Prayer Wheel—The Rosary: "The rosary hasn't died out. How many thousand Hail Marys, Our Fathers, and Glory Bes are being struck on the rosary strings at this instant across the globe? The rosary encircles the world like a magnificent Tibetan prayer wheel, spinning out adoration. It's a giant carousel you can climb upon at any point and step off again, knowing that the prayer will keep going with or without you" (Carol Zaleski, coauthor, *Prayer: A History*).

The Labyrinth: Walking the labyrinth is an ancient meditative practice that takes us to the center of our being and out again. The labyrinth is like a maze. Unlike a maze, however, it offers one path, which always leads to the center. The labyrinth is "a tool to guide healing, deepen self-knowledge, and empower creativity. Walking the labyrinth clears the mind and gives insight to the spiritual journey. It urges action. It calms people in the throes of life transitions. It helps them see their lives in the context of a path, a pilgrimage. To those who feel they have untapped gifts, it stirs the creative fires within. To those who are in deep sorrow, the walk gives solace and peace" (Dr. Lauren Artress, *Walking a Sacred Path*).

Centering Prayer: This contemplative style of prayer can be summed up in one phrase: *Be still*. It is prayer without words. The process is simple. Centering prayer involves sitting still for twenty minutes in an upright position, with your eyes closed and your hands in an open position in your lap. The prayer begins by introducing a sacred word that you have chosen (e.g. Peace, Abba, Shalom, Jesus, Yahweh). It is a symbol of your consent to God's presence and action within. When you become aware of thoughts, return *ever so gently* to your sacred word. Let go of your thoughts. Just sit. Resist no thought; entertain no thought; react to no thought; return *ever so gently* to your sacred word. At the end of twenty minutes, remain in silence for a couple more minutes to readjust to your external senses. *To learn more,* see Thomas Keating's book, *Open Mind, Open Heart* (Continuum International Publishing Group, 1994).

Find many more ways to pray in *The Way We Pray: Prayer Practices from Around the World* by Maggie Oman Shannon and *Talking to God*, ed. John Gattuso.

9

PUSH:
Pray Until Something Happens

I don't often open "forwarded" emails. Who has time? But every once in a while, I get sucked in. One day, in a weak moment, I opened up a story that has twice found its way into reflections I've given at Sunday Mass on campus! And each time, I've heard students refer to it for weeks, months, sometimes even a year after they heard it. It's that memorable a story. Recently I was sitting in the South Cathedral in Beijing not knowing what to expect from the Chinese priest's homily, when this very same story came tumbling out of his mouth in heavily Chinese-accented English. It's that *universal* a story. Just PUSH! Pray Until Something Happens. Maybe you've heard it; maybe it's *your* story!

> There once was a man who was sleeping at night in his cabin when suddenly his room filled with light and God appeared. God told the man he had work for him to do and showed him a huge rock in the front of his cabin.
>
> God explained that the man was to push against the rock with all his might. So the man did . . . day after day. For many years he worked from sun up to sundown, his shoulders set squarely against the cold, massive surface of the unmoving rock, pushing with all his might.

Each night the man returned to his cabin sore and worn out, feeling that his whole day had been spent in vain.

Since the man was showing discouragement, Satan decided to enter the picture by placing thoughts into his weary mind: "You've been pushing against that rock for a long time and it hasn't budged." He gave the man the impression that the task was impossible and that he was a failure. These thoughts discouraged and disheartened the man.

Satan said, "Why kill yourself over this? Just put in your time, giving just the minimum effort and that will be good enough." That's what the weary man planned to do but decided to make it a matter of prayer and take his troubled thoughts to God.

"God," he said, "I've labored long and hard, putting all my strength to do what you have asked. Yet, after all this time, I have not even budged that rock by half a millimeter. What's wrong? Why am I failing?"

God responded with compassion, "My friend, when I asked you to serve me and you accepted, I told you your task was to push against the rock with all of your strength which you have done. Never did I mention to you that I expected you to move it. Your task was to push. And now you have come to me with your strength spent thinking that you have failed. But is that really so?

"Look at yourself. Your arms are strong and muscled, your back sinewy and brown; your hands are calloused from constant pressure, your legs have become massive and hard. Through opposition you have grown much and your abilities now surpass what you used to have.

"True, you haven't moved the rock. But your calling was to be faithful and to push—to exercise your faith and trust my wisdom. You've done that.

"Now I, my friend, will move the rock."

It was December, the first Sunday of Advent, last time I told this story—just before final exams. The Gospel was all about end times. I said to the students:

> Usually when we talk about end times, we think literally of the end of the world. But doesn't each of us at one time or another face a situation in our life that feels like the end of the world? Our own lives sometimes feel apocalyptic. The earth of our hearts and souls is in dismay; we are perplexed by the roaring sea and waves of war, ill health, troubled relationships, situations that seem impossible to change, dreams that have been shattered. There are times when we have no control over what is happening to us . . .

I concluded by saying,

> When everything seems to go wrong, just PUSH.
> When school or work gets you down, just PUSH.
> When people don't react the way you think they should, just PUSH.
> When people just don't understand you, just PUSH.
> Push p-u-s-h. Pray Until Something Happens!
>
> Pray until something happens *for you*. Pray until something happens *for others*. Pray until there's peace on earth. Perhaps the greatest gift you can give another is to pray for them. To pray with them until something happens.

Sometimes it takes a long time for something to happen. And yet most always, out of nowhere, as Anne Lamott would say, grace arrives *eventually*.

I am reminded of a poignant scene in Liz Gilbert's best-selling book, *Eat, Pray, Love.* The decision of whether or not to divorce her husband leads her to an eerie dark night of "hopeless, life-threatening despair." Somehow it occurs to her that this is the time when others typically turn to God for help. She begins an awkward conversation with a God she doesn't know, and tells God the terrible trouble she's in. As she speaks, she begins sobbing uncontrollably. She explains that she is in desperate need of help. Her prayer narrows to one simple line that she says over and over, sobbing all the while: "Please tell me what to do . . . please tell me what to do." Mid-sob, she stops crying. Then, out of nowhere, she hears a voice that tells her simply to *"go back to bed, Liz . . . Go back to bed* because I love you. *Go back to bed* because the only thing you need for now is to get some rest and take good care of yourself . . . *Go back to bed, Liz."*[26]

My stepdaughter Julie and I frequently use Gilbert's line *"Go back to bed, Liz"* as code for letting go when we've done everything we can, for trusting God when we don't know what to do, for recognizing God's love when we're scared or depressed or overwhelmed, or for simply ending our conversation when we're just too tired to carry on. I'll say it to her, she'll say it to me: *"Go to bed, Liz."* Then we laugh and hang up. We know we've got to PUSH, but then we've really got to *go to bed!*

Recently my feisty, faith-filled eighty-nine-year-old friend, Marge, faced having no control over what was happening to her. She was in one of those situations that was impossible to change—one of those times when she needed to PUSH and PUSH hard. She was facing her own end time. She had survived ovarian cancer twenty years ago, but now Marge was dying slowly from lung cancer. Actually, she was dying quickly, but as we lived with her day to day, the dying process seemed to drag on forever. We had seen Marge at Mass on Saturday, and by the following Wednesday, she was on home-hospice care. Just forty-six days later, Marge was gone.

They told Marge this would be a painful death, and it was. They said she'd cough up blood; she did. They said that eventually she'd bleed out. It seems God spared her that. Fearful as she was of bleeding out, Marge was one brave and trusting little lady who knew how to pray until something happened. Unlike Liz Gilbert, hers was not an initial, awkward conversation with God. She knew and loved the one with whom she spoke. She was full of trust. She prayed relentlessly to be reunited with her beloved Oscar who'd been gone now for five years. She was ready to die, looked forward, in fact, to seeing God and Oscar and her parents. Besides, she had questions for them! She talked freely and mischievously about how she'd come back and surprise us after she died. People do that, you know!

But, death took its own bittersweet time. Meanwhile, Margie "held court" each day with her steady stream of visitors. She uplifted them and kept them laughing. But there were scary coughing moments, too—moments when she'd cry out "No more! Please, God, no more! Oh my God . . . no more!"

One day early on, she collapsed in my arms. I thought she was dead. Turns out, she was out of oxygen. She had removed the oxygen line from her nose so she could bathe by herself. It was too much. We dragged her back to her bed, got the oxygen reconnected, and began to pray. We were hailing Mary "now and at the hour of our death. Amen." Slowly, she came to. Eventually her smile returned. Soon as we all caught our breath, she was joking with us again, bestowing some of those wonderful and amazing "final gifts." I said to the others, I think we've just had our dress rehearsal!

As Margie was praying hard for something to happen, the "something happening" was going on all around us. Volunteer caregivers showed up around the clock for the entire forty-six days. Some would take regular daylong or nightlong shifts. Others would fill in a half day or several hours at a time here and there as they could. Her son came every weekend. Hospice personnel checked in regularly and were on call 24/7 but could only *stay* round the clock should a crisis arise.

At first Margie's neophyte caregivers were scared. Most had never taken care of a dying person before. They had never experienced someone's death. They felt uneasy about administering pain medication. But once they volunteered, they were eager to come back to spend time with Margie the way Mitch Albom did on *Tuesdays with Morrie.*

As Margie PUSHed, something was happening to her caregivers. Those who knew and loved Margie got to know others who were just getting to know and love her. People from church who simply passed each other on their way in and out of church got to see gifts they never knew each other had. Some brought food, some massage, some the giggles. Others delivered medical knowledge, hairdressing skills, bathing techniques. Some brought the Eucharist, others prayed with Margie. Each attended to Marge in their own unique way. Loving kindness got stirred up, and it was infectious. Something was happening.

Something was also happening to Margie's son. These last days of his mother's life seemed like some of the best days. The roles were reversed. As once she cared for him, he now cared for her. He felt closer to her. They talked more, reminisced more, looked at old pictures together, hung them around the room for all to see. Something was happening.

When it was my turn one Sunday night, Margie woke in the middle of the night. I always slept with one eye open, listening for any slight cough or wheeze, ready to administer her drugs and to hold her when she was scared. This night, however, was different. There was no coughing. Instead there was the restlessness that sometimes accompanies those "dark nights" of the soul. Margie couldn't sleep. She was anxious about a decision she made in love, fearful that it may have caused alienation. She wanted so desperately to make things right. We talked and prayed and talked some more—praying always that something would happen.

It's hard to know what to say to alleviate this kind of gnawing pain for which there is no drug. Somehow, as I held Marge, I thought of Corrie ten Boom, the Christian woman who hid Jews in her home during the Holocaust and who was hauled off to Ravensbrück Concentration Camp for her courageous acts of kindness.

Corrie ten Boom was released from the camp unexpectedly just before the war ended. Years later, after delivering an inspiring talk about forgiveness based on her experience at Ravensbrück, Corrie could see a man coming from the back of the room to greet her. As he approached, she suddenly recognized him as her SS guard at Ravensbrück. A rush of emotions came over her. It took everything she had to extend her hand to this man who had tormented her. She prayed, "Please, God, do for me what I cannot do for myself."

I told this story to Marge in the middle of the night. I told her how Corrie ten Boom felt a warm tingling sensation pulse through her arm as she prayed and how she was able to shake her captor's hand as he asked her to forgive him. I repeated and adapted Corrie's words to Margie: "Please, God, do for me what

I cannot do for myself. Help my son in the way I was unable to. Help me to trust you. Please do for me what I cannot do . . ." We repeated the words again and again, between Hail Marys.

I didn't say it, but I was thinking it. *"Go to bed, Liz. Go back to bed* because I love you. *Go back to bed* because the only thing you need for now is to get some rest and take good care of yourself . . . *Go back to bed, Liz." Eventually,* Margie dosed off. Her breathing was easy and restful.

Days later, Margie's pain began to spiral out of control. Even Hospice struggled to manage it. She entered what they call "the active stage of dying." The time of crisis where the hospice nurse could "stay on" had arrived. The volunteers relaxed as skilled nurses managed Marge's care. But they never stopped coming.

It was Saturday morning, my turn to be with Margie again. I had gotten a call earlier in the morning before my shift saying that she had been calling out for her sons. When I arrived, her son greeted me with the news that Margie had died just moments before I arrived. The two of us held each other the way my brother and I held each other when my mother died—sobbing, not wanting to let go.

We'd been letting go of Margie for days. Over and over, I sang to her, "May the angels come to greet you, come to meet you in paradise." It's the song we sing at church for funerals. I changed the words sometimes to "May Oscar come to greet you, come to greet you with yellow roses." We all were praying for God to take Margie home to Oscar. She had suffered enough. She was ready. Death seemed friendlier than this agony. But Margie stayed around long enough to work one last bit of magic. Love was growing all around her. From her bed, she was conducting beautiful music that will continue to linger in the hearts of all her caretakers. Something happened to us. We will never be the same.

We don't know when, if, or how the rock will be moved. But we know what beautiful things can happen in the process. And so I say from experience and with great confidence: Don't give up! The darkest hour is just before dawn. Keep going. When you get to the end of your rope, tie a knot and hang on. Always remember to "PUSH." And sometimes just *"go back to bed, Liz."*

We must receive our satisfaction from our faithfulness alone and not from results or gratitude.[27]

—Robert Wicks

There is no one who does not have to choose sometime, someway, between giving up and growing stronger as they go along. And yet, if we give up in the midst of struggle, we never find out what the struggle would have given us in the end. If we decide to endure it to the end, we come out changed by the doing of it. It is a risk of mammoth proportions. We dare the development of the self.[28]

—Joan Chittister

Me
Writing Emails after Chemo #1
New Wig, New Day!

That's My Neusy!
Beloved Caretaker

Wonderful Parents
Laura and Steve

Wonderful Family
Jer, Andrea, Diana, Steve, Lynn, Espy, David, Danielle, Alex

The Rest of the Family
Julie with Jer and Rusty
"Back East"

First Writer's Getaway
Breaking Away in NYC

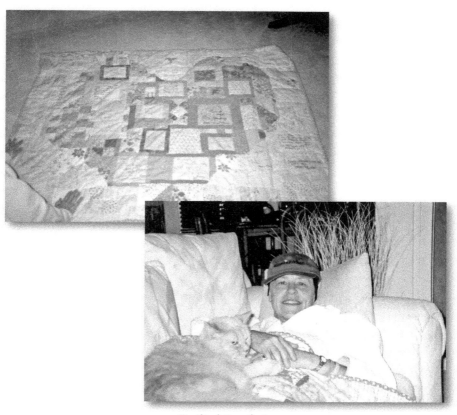

Quilted Comforts
and a Cat that Purrs!

Making Faces at Cancer!
Relay for Life at UCSD

What Kika Found
Her Mother's Sacred Space
and God Box

God Box on a Chain
Breathe in the Names

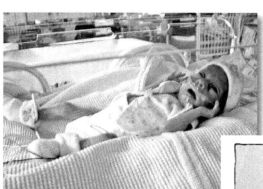

Diva Savannah
in the NICU

Savannah at 2

My Great Niece
Milan Kassia

Steve W. LeMere
February 27, 1945 - June 10, 2008

My Brother

First Anniversary
Cancer-free
I am Alive!

Create Your Own
Online God Box

10

A New Job:
God Box Facilitator

I've only held three career-related jobs in my lifetime, all in ministry, each a ten—to seventeen-year stint, each requiring leadership skills—teaching, directing, facilitating, etc. "God Box Facilitator" is one job I never heard of, dreamed of, or imagined for myself. I hadn't really thought of my role with the God Box as a job until my cousin gave me a title. He called me a "powerful prayer broker!" Though I was uncomfortable with the title for all its *power* and *brokerage* implications, it did confirm the fact that I did indeed have a new "job!"

One of the things I've learned about myself, primarily through the observations of others, is that I'm not afraid to ask. My colleague, Fr. Dominic, once told me that he was impressed by how bold I was in asking God to heal me of cancer and how bold I was in asking others to ask God to help me.

Maybe this comes from being so good at, or at least so experienced at, asking others to do things. Students often warned each other about how hard it was to resist "saying yes to Lynn" when asked to get involved. I myself began warning them to beware of talking to me for more than ten minutes because they would probably end up doing something.

I love to put people to work doing good things. It boosts their confidence, and good things get done! And I've noticed, people rather like being asked. Maybe all this has been good training for my new job.

I think it has something to do with trust. It wouldn't be easy to ask people to do things if I didn't trust that the need was worthy, or didn't trust them to recognize the importance of the need, or didn't trust they could do it. It's a lot like asking God.

Henri Nouwen says, "Our numerous requests simply become the concrete way of saying that we trust in the faithfulness of God's goodness. Whenever we pray with hope, we put our lives in the hands of God. Fear and anxiety fade away and everything we are deprived of is nothing but a finger pointing out the direction of God's hidden promise which one day we shall taste in full."[29]

My ability to ask was further strengthened on a student retreat where we "picked a promise" to live by for the year. I chose "seek and you will find; knock and the door will be opened to you" (Mt 7). We were instructed to simplify the passage, put it in our own words so we'd remember it easily, and then decorate a candle with our simple words. The words on my candle? "Just ask!"

I was drawn to this Scripture promise partly because of a story by John Shea that I read years ago.[30] It's his creative recasting of the story of the Woman at the Well from John's Gospel. In it, the Samaritan woman and Jesus are having their conversation about thirst. Jesus says: "Ask me. Ask me for a drink." And then he tells the Samaritan woman, "Thirst makes friends of us all." Ever since I read that story for the first time, those lines have been planted in my soul. Jesus told the woman, "Just ask!" I've been just asking more freely, more boldly since I first came into contact with that story! Maybe this boldness is a prerequisite for a God Box Facilitator.

So what does a *GBF* do anyway? What would someone who wanted to start a God Box for their own community actually be taking on? Here's what *I* do:

I gather the prayers of the people throughout the week from emails sent by those on my list. My list consists of two Yahoo Groups from the Catholic Community at UCSD (where I worked when this began) and a personal "God Box Group" list of 240 friends and family members. A few people's email server won't accept bulk mailings, so I keep one smaller list to accommodate them. I suppose there's a way for them to unblock their email to receive the God Box. I leave that to those more computer savvy than I!

I ask the *God Box Community* to compose their request exactly the way they would like to see it in the God Box and to submit it to me by early Monday morning. I reserve the right to edit it. Requests come in all week, with most coming in on Monday just after that week's God Box has been sent.

Throughout the week I copy and paste incoming requests into a Word document that I create for the week. I set up a folder in My Documents and label each week's God Box by date. I ask those submitting a request to put "God Box" in the subject line of their email so that I can easily spot their requests. Because I use Gmail and because most people send their requests as a response to that week's God Box, most requests are grouped into one "conversation" that is connected to my original email. That's the way Gmail works, and that's helpful! With so much incoming email, the toughest thing for me is to make sure I don't miss anyone's request. Once in a while, I do! They let me know!

On Monday morning, I scan my email one last time for requests then write a brief personal note to the group. Most of the people on my list know me. While some could do without hearing what I've been up to in the past week, most have told me that they appreciate my note because it personalizes the whole experience. There is a connection at least to me. It is different from writing a request to an organization on a Web page where no one knows your name. My challenge is to be brief, so my family tells me!

The format for the God Box emerged over time. In the beginning, I wrote the prayer intentions quite simply: please pray for so and so who has cancer, so and so who is struggling with depression, so and so who will have surgery.

Then, I began sending the whole story as it was sent to me. I know how much more connected I felt when I knew more of the story—or at least more than a one-line diagnostic. Sometimes I edit the entries—shorten them, remove some of the intricate details. I'm always concerned about imposing on people's time and energy. I want to be respectful. Sometimes I give the abbreviated story as the prayer intention and then place the rest of the story at the end for those who have more time or interest, those who know the person involved, or those know someone in a similar situation.

My friend G told me *not* to shorten things to fit our fast-paced lifestyle. "Go deeper," she said, "Let them see. Let them feel. Touch them."

Eventually, to lighten things up a bit, I followed a suggestion to add "Praise and Thanks and Updates" to the weekly email.

Then came the "List in a Nutshell." Someone wrote and asked if the names of those we were praying for could be listed at the end so they could cut out just the names and carry that little piece of paper with them. So now I include the "List in a Nutshell."

We eventually created our own "God Box" Candle page at www.gratefulness. org where candles can be lit online for those we keep in prayer. I include a hot link to it at the end of the "List in a Nutshell."

"In closing," I offer a prayer, a poem, a reflection, notes from a conference I attended—anything I think will feed my readers' souls. Early on, I decided that I wanted to offer something back to these people who open themselves up so generously each week to all the pain and suffering that filters through the God Box. I wanted to offer something that would enhance their spiritual life, lift them up.

Many tell me that this "closing" is a favorite part of the God Box. One young woman told me that she has purchased several of the books these prayers and poems come from as gifts. She was excited to know of such beautiful, contemporary, creative resources for prayer. She said this part of the God Box has helped develop her own spiritual life, and she was passing that on to others. Another young woman wrote to tell me how dried up she felt spiritually and how the prayers in the God Box stimulated her to get back on track. See for yourself what they're talking about. The "Prayers, Poems, and Reflections in the God Box" are my gift to you in chapter 13.

To summarize, here's the outline of the weekly God Box in a nutshell:

- A Personal Note
- Praise and Thanks and Updates
- This Week's Intentions
- The List in a Nutshell
- The Link to the "God Box" Candle page at www.gratefulness.org
- Closing prayer, poem, reflection

As they say, "A picture's worth a thousand words." Here's a snapshot of what the *God Box* looks like.

The God Box
June 16, 2008

Greetings Dear Friends and Family,

Quite a week. Last Tuesday at just about this time, I received the numbing news that my brother Steve had died. Since then we have been immersed in sweet remembrances, healing conversations, family and liturgical rituals, and the love and prayers of so many people. Our hearts are full and grateful.

From laughing at Steve's crazy old jokes and smoking cigars in his honor,
    to eating rich, juicy comfort foods and drinking choice red wines,
        to hearing sacred soothing texts, and singing "On Eagles' Wings" just
        like we did for Mom and Dad and Kathy and Marilyn before him,

to laughing and crying at stories that touched our hearts and lifted our spirits, we began our grieving process.

We are so grateful for your loving kindness. It has everything to do with the way we managed our way through this week. It has spoken loudly to us of the importance of relationships and faith . . . and the importance of this powerful prayer network. Thanks so much for walking through these difficult days with us.

We are shifting gears now to prepare ourselves to fly to Beijing on Thursday. Today it was all about the paperwork . . . tomorrow it will be all about the laundry and packing. We leave at 8:05 a.m. flying from San Diego to San Francisco . . . and then we fly nonstop to Beijing. We'll spend a week there and then fly on to Bangkok for 4 days. No tours, no car rental, just us and our two feet and plenty of good guidebooks to get us around to all the important sites and experiences.

As I mentioned last week, the God Box will be on vacation as well. If there's something you or I missed for this week, I will be happy to send it out tomorrow morning. After that, I encourage you to go to our Candle page to post your prayer intentions until we return on July 1.

This Week's Praise and Thanks and Updates

From Pat: Tom's balance and coordination continue to improve dramatically. He can walk alone and goes up and down stairs without assistance now, albeit stiffly. His speech is soft and deliberate yet, in part due to mild impairment in coordination of the mouth. Of greatest concern to Tom is slower processing speed, which also has improved markedly. Most of the brain swelling will subside in 4-6 weeks, with continued improvement in processing speed and speech during that time (and even up to one year). Blood resorption from the hemorrhage takes about 10–12 weeks. Tom still beats me at Scrabble and taught his speech therapist how to play Cribbage today. After his discharge, Tom will continue with outpatient speech, occupational and physical therapies three times/week on an outpatient basis.

From Angela: My system handled the chemo pretty well again this round. No horrible side effects, just the usual mouth sores. On the downside, there haven't been any positive results from this chemo. Rather than a decline, the antigen increased by 300. Obviously, I am very disappointed.

This Week's Intentions

From S. Michelle: Please remember **Marybeth**. She is a business woman, 46 years of age and has Cancer that came quickly and is moving quickly throughout her body. Thanks.

From Vinka: Please keep my sister, **Rebeca**, in the God Box for her continued healing from cancer. And please add **my mom** who fell down a long flight of stairs. Luckily, she broke no bones but has some staples in her head, a few bruises, and continued dizziness. Nevertheless she is doing quite well.

From Sister Joanette: Please pray for my dear friend **Sister Rita Mary** who received a distressing diagnosis on Friday (June 6) of Stage 4 Cancer of the Breast, which has spread to the lymph nodes in her neck. She will not know the prognosis until after having a PET Scan.

From Bill: I am reluctant to add this person to the prayer list only because in comparison, she is not ill. My prayer request goes to my number 2 daughter, **Brianne.** She leaves tomorrow, Wed., for Boston and her new adventure at Physical Therapy Graduate School. We pray that the Good Lord will keep her safe, focused and working hard on her studies. Her mentor said that she is one who needs to be in Physical Therapy. She is dedicated, people-caring, intelligent, and hardworking. Thank you for including her in the God Box.

From Renee: Please add **Ellen** to the next God Box. She'll be having her 4th knee surgery on Friday (old soccer injury). We are hoping and praying for the elimination of pain, after this surgery. Thanks for the prayer support.

For Julie whose Interstitial Cystitis treatment was postponed a week. Please surround her with your prayers next Tuesday . . . that she can handle the pain of treatment and be rewarded with relief from constant pain.

For **Diana and Andrea and all of our family and friends** who grieve the loss of my brother Steve. And for **Steve** as he enters eternal life and experiences everlasting peace.

For **Diana's sister Rosie and her friend Mary**, both of whom lost their husbands recently. For strength, courage, and peace.

For **Lani**, our dear next-door neighbor from childhood who is recovering from removal of a stage 4 brain tumor and is undergoing chemo treatments.

For **Arnie** who is dealing with both Parkinson's Disease and cancer; and for his wife **Sally** who suffers from carotid artery disease.

For **friends going through a divorce.**

For **all those suffering from tornadoes and flooding in the Midwest.**

For **peace.**

The List in a Nutshell
Pat and Tom
Angela
Marybeth
Rebeca
Vinka's Mom
Sister Rita Mary
Brianne
Ellen
Julie
Diana and Andrea, family, and friends
Steve (RIP)
Rosie
Mary
Lani
Arnie and Sally
Friends going through a divorce

Those suffering from tornadoes and flooding in the Midwest
For peace
Click here to light a candle in the God Box

In closing, I offer a poem by Joyce Rupp from *Out of the Ordinary:*

Leaning on the Heart of God

Accept the strength that comes
from the grace of Christ Jesus [2 Timothy 2:1]

I am leaning on the heart of God.
I am resting there in silence.
All the turmoil that exhausts me is brought to bear on this great love.

No resistance or complaint is heard as I lean upon God's welcome.
There is gladness for my coming.
There is comfort for my pain.

I lean, and lean, and lean upon this heart that hurts with me.
Strength lifts the weight of my distress.
Courage wraps around my troubles.

No miracle of instant recovery.
No taking away life's burdens.
Yet, there is solace for my soul, and refuge for my exiled tears.

It is enough for me to know the heart of God is with me, full of mercy and compassion,
tending to the wounds I bear.

Until July . . .
Love and hugs,
Lynn =)

11

From One *GBF* to Another

Perhaps you'd like to become a GBF and start your own God Box Community. You could begin with the format I use, or perhaps your own creativity will suggest something else. Play with it. Let the style emerge as you get feedback from those on your list. Because there's no copyright here, you can do whatever works best for you. Design it with your community in mind. Let your own personality shine through. Before you begin, though, you might want to check out what I've learned from doing the God Box over a period of time.

It is important to protect the Internet privacy of the people on your list. I finally got into the good habit of sending the emails to myself with blind copies *(Bcc)* to the rest. There's just too much spamming going on out there not to protect the readers. This is not a problem with Yahoo! Groups or others like them because the names on those "subscription" services never appear.

The personal privacy of the one submitting a request needs to be protected. People differ greatly in how much they want to tell about their personal lives, and that needs to be respected. Sometimes it is just too painful or too difficult to expose the vivid details of one's physical or mental health. Sometimes it's a matter of honesty versus candor in asking for prayers. Knowing how much to say can be a tough call sometimes.

It's always an option to leave names out or to place an anonymous petition. It does occur to me that someone's anonymous petition may not be something I'd pray for. For example, I may not want to pray that someone else's candidate win an election! God knows my heart, and I feel confident that God can do the filtering! Conflict of interest in prayer is something God deals with all the time.

Personal pieties vary greatly. I am picky about what I include as prayers, poems or reflections in the God Box. I try to appeal to a broad spectrum of readers without compromising my own integrity. Of course, my own personal spirituality shines through. I am a Catholic Christian as are most of my readers. I don't hide that. Yet I do offer prayers from other traditions. I include both traditional and contemporary prayers. I include things that may be a stretch for some readers but hopefully won't alienate them.

Sometimes things come in late, yet the prayers are needed *now*. And then I have a decision to make! When someone's surgery is *today* and the God Box has just gone out, I don't like to wait until next week to ask for prayers, nor do they! I remember how I ran to all my friends when I was first diagnosed with cancer and how good it felt to know their love and prayers were surrounding me. It's no fun being in the trenches *alone*! There's something about putting our fears and hopes in someone else's hands that helps us relax a bit. It's like that candle that keeps burning for us while we continue our daily tasks. It helps us let go because we feel we've done something. So while I want to respond to the urgency of those who run to the God Box with their requests, I also don't want to pepper the God Box community with too many emails. Neither do I wish to play into a mentality that prayer is magic or that God doesn't hear unless there's a chorus. I do my best to make good judgments. I'm sure some would make a different call than I do sometimes.

Suffering builds a bridge. When I first began sharing details of my cancer diagnosis in emails, I recoiled a bit, wondering why I'd want to do that. Then I'd get feedback saying, "More, more! You should write this for a broader audience!" There's something about getting inside someone else's story. Sometimes we identify personally with it. Sometimes we thank God it's not about us. Sometimes we simply recognize how fragile life is and commit ourselves to living more fully, with an attitude of gratitude.

As we watch how others respond to situations, we can't help but ask ourselves what our own response would be. How would *I* deal with this? What is it that's giving this person hope, strength, courage? Listening to another's story nudges us toward our own self-reflection.

The wisdom of the God Box says that those who "put it all out there" touch others who have gone through a similar struggle and who now stand ready to support, listen, be with them in their struggle. I often get offers to help from those who have "been there" or who are "the experts in the field."

One vivid personal example of that is when my brother was having a difficult time being diagnosed. He would get out of breath easily and could hardly climb a flight of stairs. He had recently had heart surgery, and now a new angiogram showed no blockages. The doctors were settling on a diagnosis of acid reflux! We knew there was more to it. I put a note in the God Box asking people to pray that the doctors would discover what was wrong. A note came flying back from a heart specialist who is a member of the Catholic Community at UCSD. He offered a second opinion. My brother leaped at the opportunity and within a week had a new diagnosis of "constrictive pericarditis," this doctor's specialty! Just week's later, he had the surgery to remove this "boa constrictor" that was squeezing his heart, and he could breathe again. Ahhhhh . . .

People also see themselves in other people's prayer intention. What was too difficult to ask for themselves, they see someone else asking for. It ratchets up their own courage a notch. Someone else had the same problem. Someone else dared to ask for help. It's OK to ask.

People often wonder if their intention is *worthy* of being placed in the God Box. They feel that, in the scheme of things, their need seems puny, unimportant. I've had college students tell me that they feel foolish placing a prayer for a good MCAT result in the God Box because there are such greater needs in the world. I tell them that nothing is too little or too unimportant. God is capable of hearing it all. God loves us all and is interested in everything we're about. God is capable of working with and for us all. While an MCAT score may not be life-threatening (at least not to others), it is the scary reality of one wishing to get into medical school. It is worthy of God's attention. It is worthy of the community's prayer.

Probably one of the most important characteristics of one who facilitates this kind of God Box is a willingness to develop their own spirituality, their own prayer life. It's impossible to give what you do not have. I spend time at prayer within a community, with my husband, and by myself. I keep up a regular routine of daily Mass, meditation, spiritual reading, participation in a faith-sharing group, and being with those in need. That feeds me and gives me something to share with others.

How much time does it take to do the God Box? People ask me that all the time! Of course that varies depending on the number of requests that come in, whether I've kept up with pasting them into a Word document during the week, how quickly I decide on the prayer or poem for the closing, and what I decide to tell folks about my week. I like to think that this takes about an hour on Mondays, but I can assure you that it takes much longer some weeks! Sometimes I get lost in my own reflections about my week. Sometimes I get lost in selecting the closing prayer or poem. I usually write a quick note back to folks letting them know their prayer request arrived and assuring them that I have already begun praying for them. Sometimes I write a personal note to comfort the one who is struggling deeply with the concern for which they are seeking prayers. It all takes time. To me it is a ministry of care that I feel called to do. I just do it, no matter how long it takes. And as I work, I keep my candle burning as my way of praying for those in that week's God Box.

Perhaps you will launch your own God Box prayer network for your church, religious community, campus ministry, or family. Or perhaps you'd just like to participate in something that is already set up. Chapter 12 provides some options.

What would you say about **the** *God Box?*
The Community responds.

❖ I love sharing in your life at the beginning of The God Box. I appreciate the suggestions and news and gifts you give me, like the gratefulness.org Web site.

❖ I love the sense of community it promotes. The prayers at the end of each God Box are a perfect way to conclude the week's intentions.

❖ I like how the requests are mostly kept in the requestor's own words.

❖ I do enjoy when people write updates and let you know the good news too. Sometimes all the unfortunate news is a bit overwhelming. I love the inspirationals. I even copy them in a folder and have used them before my anatomy class.

❖ I have been sued for malpractice, and the trial will start at the end of April. I believe we will win, but this is the first time this has happened to me, and it is very stressful. I need the support of the community in this but not sure how to present it. My feeling is to be straightforward and just say that my trial for malpractice starts in April and to ask for prayers for all involved. Is this too much information? On the other hand, I think people should understand that there are serious problems associated with being a physician. For example, because of this trial, I will not be able to see patients or teach for three or four weeks while I attend the trial. *(We did leave his name out, and* yes, *he did win! Cause for celebration in our Praise and Thanks and Updates!)*

❖ I like that we always give thanks first. I like hearing the news of the progress for the people we prayed for, even if it's not always positive. Reading a little about the person beyond the prayer for that particular need helps me to see the extent of that person's situation.

❖ When I get the God Box, sometimes I have intentions to pray for but just don't get around to sending to you. Sometimes the stories are too long, and I don't know how to compose the email. For example, I prayed today for my coworker whose father died suddenly and unexpectedly two Fridays ago. Her family is from Jamaica and was visiting their son in New York to meet their one-year-old twin grandbabies. Her dad died in New York early in the trip. We think he was only sixty years old. He was very close to his daughter, my coworker. She flew up there, and the family, in their grief, had to deal with getting all of them and her dad back to Jamaica and then plan the funeral. My coworker is such an interesting person. She went through RCIA at an African American Catholic parish here in Durham during grad school (at around age thirty). Small blessings are that she spent a nice trip with her parents in early January in Jamaica.

❖ The follow-ups are nice and especially when we see someone doing well as a result of our prayers. We like the summary of names you recap at the end.

❖ I need the good news section; it is important to be able to celebrate healings. And a reflective prayer or reading at the end helps pull things together.

❖ I would add a very short but sweet opening prayer . . . just to start the conversation . . . since to me that is what it is.

❖ I would not change anything, except to have requesters' email addresses included, which would help me once in a while in responding to a few.

❖ I look forward to it every week, although anticipating that at least a portion of it will contain bad/sad news. That too has a positive side; in that I am reminded weekly to count my blessings! I cannot claim to search often for spiritual or inspirational reading material unless led to same by someone whose faith I admire. So . . . I very much appreciate that you attach spiritual writings to your weekly messages!

❖ It has opened my eyes more to what those with cancer live with. Within my family I have experienced heart disease, but not cancer. It has also provided me other avenues of prayer through other Web sites that I was not aware of.

My Gift to You:
Hope Strength Courage
@ Your Fingertips

12

Sacred Space in Cyberspace

Cyberspace can become sacred space. But sometimes, it helps to have a navigator! Here are some of the websites that have been particularly valuable to me or that have had significantly broad appeal. At these sites you'll find resources for prayer, opportunities to participate in prayer circles, places to submit prayer requests, and resources for developing your own spiritual life.

> *What is happening through the use of the Internet is that it is becoming sanctified and making the airwaves holy, not only the mundane, but even the spiritual realm—realms [used] for godly purposes, divine purposes.*[31]
>
> –Rabbi Krinsky

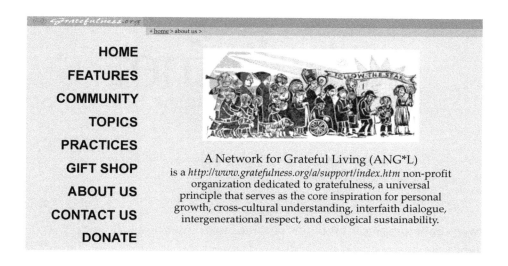

Gratefulness.org

+ home > about us >

HOME

FEATURES

COMMUNITY

TOPICS

PRACTICES

GIFT SHOP

ABOUT US

CONTACT US

DONATE

A Network for Grateful Living (ANG*L) is a *http://www.gratefulness.org/a/support/index.htm* non-profit organization dedicated to gratefulness, a universal principle that serves as the core inspiration for personal growth, cross-cultural understanding, interfaith dialogue, intergenerational respect, and ecological sustainability.

www.gratefulness.org is the place participants in the God Box go to light candles online for their intentions. Anyone can light candles at gratefulness. org by clicking on "Features" and then "Candles." If you begin your own God Box, you can set up a page specifically for your group.

Besides the Candle page, I love going to **"Angels of the Hours"** (also found by clicking on "Features"). Here you can spend a minute or two throughout the day praying online accompanied by Gregorian chant. Sweet refreshment at your fingertips!

You'll also find **"Practices for Grateful Living"** which include four-step reflections on things like Water, Grief and Gratefulness, Finding Gratitude through the Labyrinth, and Harvesting the Past for Gratitude. **"Topics"** to explore include Caring for the Earth, Fear/Peace, Grief/Joy, Loneliness/ Belonging.

Tasteful **E-cards** are available at this site as well as poetry selections, book suggestions, an interfaith, multicultural calendar of feasts and remembrances, and a "Word for the Day."

Gratefulness.org is the Web site of Br. David Steindl-Rast, author of Gratefulness, the Heart of Prayer.

There is one thing stronger than all the armies in the world, and that is an idea whose time has come.

—*Victor Hugo*

www.beliefnet.com At this site, you can create a prayer circle or find one in which to participate. You can also find support groups online for things like chronic pain, cancer, depression. The site has a prayer library with resources related to comfort, depression, healing hope, loneliness, and loss. Many people have set up pages for particular causes, such as *world peace, grief, employment, infertility, etc.* You can subscribe to their "daily inspiration on the go," which can be sent directly to your cell phone.

About Beliefnet *(from their Web site):* Our mission is to help people like you find and walk a spiritual path that will bring comfort, hope, clarity, strength, and happiness.

Whether you're exploring your own faith or other spiritual traditions, we provide you inspiring devotional tools, access to the best spiritual teachers and clergy in the world, thought-provoking commentary, and a supportive community.

Beliefnet is the largest spiritual Web site. We are independent and not affiliated with any spiritual organization or movement. Our only agenda is to help you meet your spiritual needs.

Beliefnet has business or editorial partnerships with Time, ABC News, Yahoo, Chicken Soup for the Soul, Hay House, Sounds True, AmericanCatholic.org, and others.

www.spiritualityandpractice.com Whenever I visit this Web site, I tend to get stuck for at least an hour! It's that rich and diverse! I love their book and movie reviews and their practical suggestions for growing into spiritual practices from A-Z (attention . . . beauty . . . joy . . . kindness . . . peace . . . transformation . . . zeal). They offer E-courses on Practicing Spirituality with the World's Religions or with Master Teachers (such as Joan Chittister, Henri Nouwen, The Dalai Lama, Jesus, Pema Chodron, Thich Nhat Hanh, Thomas Merton, Thomas Moore . . .) or Practicing Spirituality in Places and Activities (such as at work, at home, during illness, in nature, through creativity . . .). Online retreats open possibilities for learning a classic practice such as Lectio Divina.

Here's how they describe themselves on their Web site:

This Web site, created by Frederic and Mary Ann Brussat, is devoted to resources for spiritual journeys. The site's name reflects a basic understanding: *spirituality* and *practice* are the two places where all the world's religions and spiritual paths come together. With respect for the differences among them, we celebrate what they have in common.

The Homepage gives you an overview of the rich diversity of content on the site. To the right is an **alphabet of thirty-seven essential practices of the spiritual life.** Click on any practice in the alphabet, and you'll go to its home page where you'll find ideas on how to practice using books, films, prayers, daily exercises, journals, imagery, art, music, and more. Read a definition of the practice and some of the reasons it might be a good one for you. Try a simple spiritual exercise for a concrete experience of the practice. Dip into some teaching stories and book excerpts.

The **Spiritual Practices** section includes articles and instructions on a wide variety of practices—tried-and-true methods used in the world's religions and also those simple things you do as you go along life's sacred journey.

Praying Each Day

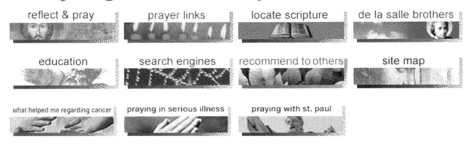

www.prayingeachday.org is a prayer and education site of the De La Salle Brothers in Great Britain.

"Reflect and Pray" gives reflections and prayers for each day of the year.

"Prayer Links," offers one hundred additional prayers as well as Web sites related to "art and icon," "prayer," "collective worship," "religious education," and other "resources."

"Locate Scripture," provides descriptions of events in the Old Testament with passage references. You'll find New Testament listings by event, Jesus' teachings, parables, and miracles.

Sacred Space

HTTP://WWW.SACREDSPACE.IE/

As described on their Web site: Sacred Space is a work of the Irish Province of the Society of Jesus. It originated in the offices of the Jesuit Communication Centre in Ireland in 1999. Being a ministry of the Irish Jesuits, it is inspired by the spirituality of Saint Ignatius of Loyola (Ignatian spirituality). Offered in twenty-two languages.

We invite you to make a "Sacred Space" in your day and spend ten minutes, praying here and now, as you sit at your computer, with the help of on-screen guidance and scripture chosen specially every day.

Sacred Space offers these "Chapels" as places that you can come to pray.

The Chapel of Intentions is where you can post public prayers. Some of these prayers are published online, a list is sent weekly to praying communities.

The Chapel of Remembrance is to help you in your prayer for the departed. You can personalize the prayers with the names of your own loved ones, creating your own prayer list.

The daily prayer practice offered at *Sacred Space* includes a brief prayer, the Gospel of the day, a reflective question that applies the passage to daily living, an option to click if you "need inspiration," and a closing prayer.

unity

www.unity.org

From Prayer Circles to a Worldwide Ministry of Peace

As described on their Web site:

Unity is a not-for-profit organization based on the teachings of Jesus and the healing power of prayer.

Our prayer, publishing, education, and retreat ministries allow us to provide people around the world with positive, spiritual messages of hope, healing, prosperity, and peace.

The Unity approach to prayer is affirmative, based on positive prayers and affirmations that have universal, interfaith appeal.

Silent Unity is available 24/7 ready to offer you free confidential prayer support whenever you want it.

Call: 1-800-NOW-PRAY (1-800-669-7729)

Write: Silent Unity, 1901 NW Blue Parkway, Unity Village, MO 64065

I have been reading the Daily Word, *published by Unity Village, for over twenty years, ever since I first received it as a gift from a friend. The positive affirmations related to healing were particularly helpful to me as I went through treatment for cancer. Reflections from the Daily Word are often used and appreciated in* the God Box. *You can subscribe to the Daily Word at the address above or find the daily reflections on their Web site day by day. Go to www.unityonline.org.*

www.worldprayers.org *According to their Web site:* The mission of The World Prayers Project is to improve human relations by celebrating the many forms of prayer and honoring the benefits of spiritual, cultural, and natural diversity.

The World Prayers Project is a 501(c) (3) nonprofit, educational, public service organization whose founding objective is to gather and present historic and contemporary world prayers in a unified, multifaith archive on the Internet.

Thousands of prayers a day are being sent across the digital network from our Web site to people visiting from over a hundred nations. As the Internet and its supporting technologies become available to more and more people throughout the world, so will our sphere of positive influence expand.

Guiding Principle. The World Prayers archive attempts to be representative of all life-affirming faiths and spiritual practices without preference to any one. It is our goal to make these great words available to everyone for study and appreciation. The prayers have been intuitively divided into four categories for the purpose of organization and navigation.

ADORATIONS
Prayers of devotion, surrender, love, praise and offering.

CELEBRATIONS
Prayers of thanksgiving, initiation, affirmation and blessing.

INVOCATIONS
Prayers of petition, supplication, calling forth and healing.

MEDITATIONS
Prayers of reflection, contemplation, being and teaching.

A fun feature of this Web site is the "Spin Our Prayer Wheel" option. With the click of a mouse, you can see what turns up for you on a given day. And if it doesn't touch your heart, spin again!

The Merton Institute
For Contemplative Living

www.mertoninstitute.org

From their Web site:

WELCOME to the Merton Institute for Contemplative Living, a valuable resource for your contemplative spiritual journey. The Institute is dedicated to

Awakening interest in contemplative living through the works of Thomas Merton to promote Merton's vision for a just and peaceful world.

WHAT DIFFERENTIATES US

What differentiates our services (programs, publications, and retreats) is Thomas Merton and his approach to contemplative living. This approach is born of deep monastic tradition and bridges this sacred orientation to secular everyday life.

The Merton Institute offers a weekly reflection from the works of Thomas Merton that you can subscribe to online.

13

Prayers, Poems, Reflections in the God Box

Seems I've always collected "messages to live by." When I was just out of college, setting up my first apartment, I couldn't afford fancy-framed artwork for the walls, so I decorated them with colorful images from magazines and calendars. Sometimes, because my French teacher taught me to love the impressionists, I'd throw in a print from the Chicago Art Museum, a Picasso or a Rouault. Next to these colored pages or on top of them, I'd paste quotes from poets, mystics, and prophets who inspired me. My roommate let me know that she couldn't even go to the bathroom without coming face to face with some message to live by!

I still collect things that inspire me—stories and prayers, poems and songs, notes and ideas. I don't plaster the walls with them anymore, but they are always at my fingertips. I surround myself with binders, files, and bookcases filled to the brim with things I love. I use them in my own quiet moments, I use them with groups, and I pass them on by email, in birthday cards, or as gifts. Something in me has always wanted to share the inspiration I've found. So when I began writing emails to the people who were praying me through cancer, it was natural for me to include something meaningful and uplifting.

These are the words of hope, strength, and courage that have nurtured participants in the *God Box*—little jewels that were doled out, one at a time, over a period of years. These are the things that have helped create sacred space in cyberspace. To enjoy them fully, you'll want to slow down here. Perhaps keep this little book at your bedside, near your morning coffee or in your briefcase. Take your time, breathe in, breathe out. Prayers are arranged by theme:

- Gratitude

- Healing

- Hope and Trust

- Love and Compassion

- Peace

- Seasons

- Suffering Death

- Miscellaneous

Gratitude

"To be grateful is to recognize the Love of God in everything He has given us — and He has given us everything. Every breath we draw is a gift of His love, every moment of existence is a grace, for it brings with it immense graces from Him. Gratitude therefore takes nothing for granted, is never unresponsive, is constantly awakening to new wonder and to praise of the goodness of God. For the grateful person knows that God is good, not by hearsay but by experience. And that is what makes all the difference."

—Thomas Merton, in *Words of Gratitude*,
Robert A. Emmons and Joanna Hill

"Spend time in silence and solitude as a way of feeling at ease, loved and free .... Where will you find a place to sit in silence and solitude, wrapped in gratitude?"

—Robert Wicks, *Everyday Simplicity*, 86–87.

Mindfulness Practice: Each morning when you put on your watch, take a good look at it with gratitude for another day and contemplate how you will fill it with love and light.

From *Seven Sacred Pauses*
Macrina Wiederkehr, 51, 56

"At dawn I have the potential of becoming a living morning praise. With my glance I give praise. With my breath I give praise. With my grateful heart I give praise. In honoring the sorrows of life, I give praise. In celebrating the joy of the moment, I give praise. My desire to live this day well gives praise. With my voice I give praise. With my silence I give praise."

"Set the clock of your heart for dawn's arrival.
Taste the joy of being awake."

i thank You God for most this amazing
E. E. Cummings

i thank You God for most this amazing
day:for the leaping greenly spirits of trees
and a blue true dream of sky; and for everything
which is natural which is infinite which is yes

(i who have died am alive again today,
and this is the sun's birthday; this is the birth
day of life and of love and wings: and of the gay
great happening illimitably earth)

how should tasting touching hearing seeing
breathing any—lifted from the no
of all nothing—human merely being
doubt unimaginable You?

(now the ears of my ears awake and
now the eyes of my eyes are opened)

Waken In Me a Gratitude for My Life
Guerrillas of Grace, Ted Loder, 76

O God, complete the work you have begun in me.
Release through me
   a flow of mercy and gentleness that will bring
   water where there is desert,
   healing where there is hurt,
   peace where there is violence,
   beauty where there is ugliness,
   justice where there is brokenness,
   beginnings where there are dead-ends.
Waken in me
   gratitude for my life,

love for every living thing,
joy in what is human and holy,
praise for you.
Renew my faith that you are God
beyond my grasp
but within my reach;
past my knowing
but within my searching;
disturber of the assured,
assurer of the disturbed;
destroyer of illusions,
creator of dreams;
source of silence and music,
sex and solitude
light and darkness
death and life.
O Keeper of Promises,
composer of grace,
grant me
glee in my blood,
prayer in my heart,
trust at my core,
songs for my journey,
and a sense of your kingdom

I Praise You for What is Yet to Be

Guerrillas of Grace, Ted Loder, 36

Wondrous Worker of Wonders,
I praise you
not alone for what has been,
or for what is,
but for what is yet to be,
for you are gracious beyond all telling of it.

I praise you
that out of the turbulence of my life
  a kingdom is coming,
    is being shaped even now
      out of my slivers of loving,
        my bits of trusting,
        my sprigs of hoping,
        my tootles of laughing,
        my drips of crying,
        my smidgens of worshipping;
that out of my songs and struggles,
    out of my griefs and triumphs,
      I am gathered up and saved,
for you are gracious beyond all telling of it.

I praise you
that you turn me loose
    to go with you to the edge of now and maybe,
      to welcome the new,
        to see my possibilities,
          to accept my limits,
and yet begin living to the limit
    of passion and compassion
    until,
      released by joy,
I uncurl to other people
  and to your kingdom coming,
for you are gracious beyond all telling of it.

A Prayer of Gratitude
May I Have This Dance? Joyce Rupp, 151–152

We are grateful for eyes that can see and ponder, for taste buds that know the sensuous pleasures of eating and drinking, for hands that hold and touch and feel, for ears that can delight in music and the voice of a friend, for a nose that can smell the aroma of newly mown grass or delicious food, and can also breathe the air that gives us life.

We are grateful for the treasure of loved ones whose hearts of openness and acceptance have encouraged us to be who we are. We are grateful for their faithfulness, for standing by us when our weaknesses stood out glaringly, for being there when we were most in need and for delighting with us in our good days and our joyful seasons.

We are grateful for the eyes of faith, for believing in the presence of God, giving us hope in our darkest days, encouraging us to listen to our spirit's hunger, and reminding us to trust in the blessings of God's presence in our most empty days.

We are grateful for the ongoing process of becoming who we are, for the seasons within, for the great adventure of life that challenges and comforts us at one and the same time.

We are grateful for the messengers of God—people, events, written or spoken words—that came to us at just the right time and helped us to grow.

We are grateful for God calling us to work with our gifts, grateful that we can be of service and use our talents in a responsible and just way.

We are grateful that we have the basic necessities of life, that we have the means and the ability to hear the cries of the poor and to respond with our abundance.

We are grateful for the miracle of life, for the green of our earth, for the amazing grace of our history; we are grateful that we still have time to decide the fate of the world by our choices and our actions, grateful that we have it within our power to bring a divided world to peace.

Faithful God, you have lavished us with love. Keep us ever mindful that you keep your promises. On our difficult days help us to remember that you are a refuge for those who need shelter, a comfort for those who feel empty and poor in spirit. On our joyful days fill us with a deep sense of thanksgiving as we experience your everlasting love. Help us to share your graciousness with all those who need a touch of generous love. AMEN.

Monday Morning Prayer
Prayers for the Domestic Church, Ed Hays, *137*

Lord, my God,
      the morning sky announces a new day.
All around me, creation is beginning its song of praise.
I now join my heart and body
      with all peoples and all creation
      as I lift up my heart to You, my God.

This day will hold much for me,
      and so that I may not miss its hidden message,
Your Word to me,
      I now enter the cave of my heart
      and, there, pray to You in stillness.
Quiet of body and peaceful of spirit,
      I rest in You.

Container of Divine Love
Out of the Ordinary, Joyce Rupp, 230.

God of affection, devotion, passion, tenderness, and all forms of love, this day we thank you for the myriad ways that we have been given a touch of your goodness. We thank you for your many beneficent gestures:
    . . . love that draws us to friendship and fidelity
    . . . love that leads us to kindness and compassion,
    . . . love that stirs in our flesh and dances in our bones,
    . . . love that lures us toward the sacred and serene,
    . . . love that calls us to new vision and growth,
    . . . love that soothes our heartaches and gentles our pain,
    . . . love that sees worth in each human being,

... love that believes in us and whispers with hope,
... love that sings in the seasons and sighs in the wind,
... love that taps on the door of forgiveness,
... love that longs for peace among all humankind,
... love that surprises and fills us with awe,
... love that sings praise for the face of earth's beauty,
... love that offers the hand of warm welcome,
... love that respects those who won't come too near,
... love that urges us to take risks and have courage,
... love that goes out to those from afar,
... love that embraces the shadow in us,
... love that sheds the old skin and welcomes the new,
... love that ripens our souls for the final journey home.

Source of Love, we offer thanks for how you are abiding in all of these forms of love. May the hearts we give and receive this Valentine's Day remind us of you, the One Great Heart, holding us all in the tenderness of your love.

From *The Haunt of Grace: Responses to the Mystery of God's Presence*, Ted Loder, 23–24

"What's enough? Countless times I've watched the sun rise like God's tender mercy to gently lift the dark blanket from the earth, and countless more times I've watched the sun set in such a splendiferous farewell that it must reflect the fringe on God's robe. I've seen the sky define blue and endless. I've watched rivers run to the sea, full as life runs to God. I've felt the sea roll in on the eternal note of mystery and assurance.

"I've scratched the ears of dogs, laughed at the ballet of cats. I've heard the cry and gurgle of the newborn, played with children, rocked with grandmothers, learned from hundreds of teachers, some of them homeless, poor, and uneducated. I've been enlarged ten times squared by writers from Shakespeare to Toni Morrison, and yet countless other storytellers, some in delis and diners, taverns and buses, churches, curb sides and prison cells.

"I have tasted bread and wine, hot dogs and caviar, somehow in the alchemy of need and gift and joy, all made holy as God's own overflowing banquet. I've been loved and forgiven beyond all deserving, and all breath to tell of it, by family and friends and God.

"I've been shaken, changed, and blessed a thousand times—and still—by the prophets, and by Christ. I've felt the touch of God, each time before I realized that's what it was. I've been shrunk and stretched at the same time by the scatter of stars and found North in one of them. I've experienced the loneliness of freedom and being human and having hard choices. I've known the thrill of small triumphs, the instruction of painful defeats, and so the amazement of being part of the incredible human pilgrimage from Adam and Eve to the twenty-first century. I've shared in the cantankerous yet remarkable family of faith called the church. I'm conscious of being conscious and alive. And all thats just for starters.

"How much does it take to praise God? I have a couple of trips around the Milky Way past enough for that, no matter if I never receive another thing. So I best get on with it . . . and praise God that I can."

From The Dalai Lama

"Every day, think as you wake up, today I am fortunate to be alive, I have a precious human life, I am not going to waste it. I am going to use all my energies to develop myself, to expand my heart out to others; to achieve enlightenment for the benefit of all beings. I am going to have kind thoughts towards others, I am not going to get angry or think badly of others. I am going to benefit others as much as I can."

From *Seven Sacred Pauses*
Macrina Weiderkehr, 71, 79

"In the middle of my morning's work, I break for blessings: a deep breath, a glance out the window, a graceful stretch, a remembrance of God, a brief reflection on the nobility of work, an encouraging word, a grateful thought, a smile, a short prayer, a remembrance of who I am, a sip of freshly brewed coffee. I honor the wisdom of pausing. The day, still young, is fresh with the dew of possibilities. My work, too, is bright with potential. When I have the wisdom to step away from work momentarily, I am able to see it as a gift for the entire world. A short, refreshing pause can enhance my growing awareness that all work has the potential of becoming love made visible—a blessing. this is the spirit's hour. I sense the overshadowing presence of all that is holy, and I remember that I am God's temple on earth, a channel for loving service. I hold out my hands to receive the blessings of the moment. When I remember to pause, blessings appear. I break for blessings."

"O Spirit of the Circling Hours.
Work through me that I may be your love poured out."

Magnificat (inclusive language) Luke 1:46–55
As used by the Cistercians of Tarrawarra Abbey *(Australia)* and Kopua *(New Zealand).*

My soul glorifies the Lord,
my spirit rejoices in God, my Saviour.
God looks on the lowliness of his servant
henceforth all ages will call me blessed.
The Almighty works marvels for me.
Holy is God's name!
There is mercy from age to age,
on those who fear God,
God puts forth his arm in strength
scattering the proud-hearted;
casts the mighty from their thrones,
raising the lowly,
fills the starving with good things,
sending the rich away empty.
God protects Israel, his servant,
remembering his mercy,
the mercy promised to our forbears,
for Abraham and his heirs for ever.

Praise the Father, the Son and Holy Spirit,
for ever and ever. Amen.

Make space in your life . . .
Everyday Simplicity, Robert Wicks, 50

"Catch yourself in the act of worrying or complaining and let go of preoccupations and unfinished business which is filling our lives. Let there be room to receive God's new, fresh gifts by appreciating what is in your life now and trusting that you will always be gifted in some way in the future. Remember the only thing you can keep forever is God's love. And, when you do try to possess persons and things, you hurt your ability to fully enjoy them while you have them in life."

From G. K. Chesterton in *Different Seasons,* Dale Turner

"You say grace before meals. All right. But I say grace before the concert and the opera, and grace before the play and pantomime, and grace before I open a book, and grace before sketching, painting, and swimming, fencing, boxing, walking, playing, dancing, and grace before I dip the pen in ink."

Healing

A Blessing Prayer for Healing
Out of the Ordinary, Joyce Rupp, 78

(keeping in mind those for whom we pray . . .)
May you desire to be healed.
May what is wounded in your life be restored to good health.
May you be receptive to the ways in which healing needs to happen.
May you take good care of yourself.
May you extend compassion to all that hurts within your body, mind, and spirit.
May you be patient with the time it takes to heal.
May you be aware of the wonders of your body, mind, and spirit and their amazing capacity to heal.
May the skills of all those who are caring for you be used to the best of their ability in returning you to good health.
May you be open to receive from those who extend kindness, care, and compassion to you.
May you rest peacefully under the sheltering wings of divine love, trusting in this gracious presence.
May you find little moments of beauty and joy to sustain you.
May you keep hope in your heart.

Hold your hands over your own heart and remember the power of love within you. Then extend your hands of love toward the one who needs healing. Give this healing love to the one being blessed. If blessing oneself, recognize and accept this power of love within you.

*If praying for oneself, insert "I" instead of "you."

Daily Word, April 7, 2006
I pray in faith and know that all is well

Praying for others, I affirm that the healing, guiding presence of God is within us all and I give thanks for our spiritual oneness. Affirming wholeness, abundance and peace for my loved ones, I have greater peace of mind about them.

To grow even further in my realization of God's presence, I pray for those I may not know well but whom I do know need to be supported in prayer. Turning within quietly, I renew my understanding of the universal nature of God.

I expand my consciousness by praying for all people of the world: the citizens, business leaders, political leaders, and those in service to their countries, supporting a world of peace.

Renewed in my own heart and soul, I pray in faith and know that all is well.

"The prayer of faith will save the sick, and the Lord will raise them up" (James 5:15).

A Blessing Prayer
(author unknown)

May the God of healing
    protect and console you.
May God grant you
    the health, help and hope you seek.
May God look upon you
    with kindness and compassion.
May God shelter you,
    and bring you solace.
May God surround you with angels
    to shield you from evil.
May God come to your aid
    with healing grace.
May God care for you,
    body, mind and spirit.
May God gladden your heart
    and transform your hurt into joy.
May God refresh and renew you.
May God hear your prayers,
    those spoken and unspoken.
May God, the giver of all good gifts,

> provide for you
> and supply all your needs.
> May God lead you to a healing place,
> to find solace and hope
> in this hurting world.
> May you always praise God
> from whom all blessings flow,
> now and forever.

Prayer for A Friend Who Is Sick
Prayers for the Domestic Church, Edward M. Hays, 169

Lord our God, hear our prayer as we come before you.
Your servant . . . is sick
   and in need of our affection
   and prayerful support.
We pause now and, in silence, pray for his (her) recovery.

   (silent prayer)

We pray for those who love . . .
   and who surround him (her) at this time of sickness.

Support them
   with the Sacred Strength of your Spirit
   so that by their love
   they may be medicine for the healing of their loved
      one.

May this sickness be for us a cause of gratitude,
   we who are enjoying the fruits of good health.
As we pray for our dear friend,
   may we also thank You
   for this fragile gift of health
   that we possess by Your Holy Will.

God, in Communion of Love,
   we now reach out (across the miles)
   and surround the bed and the body of . . .
   with light, love and the power of prayer.

    (period of silence)

Healing, health and holiness be his (hers)
May peace, grace and love surround him (her)
   and an awareness of Your Divine Presence
   be a tent over his (her) bed of pain.

Blessed are You, Lord and God,
   who rescues those You love
   from pain and sickness.

Amen

A Prayer for the World
Rabbi Harold S. Kushner

   Let the rain come and wash away
   the ancient grudges, bitter hatreds,
   held and nurtured over generations.
   Let the rain wash away
   the memory of the hurt, the neglect.
   Then let the sun come out
   and fill the sky with rainbows.
   Let the warmth of the sun heal us
   wherever we are broken.
   Let it burn away the fog
   so that we can see each other clearly.
   Let the warmth and brightness of the sun
   melt our selfishness.
   and let the light of the sun be so strong

that we will see all people as our neighbors.
Let the earth, nourished by rain,
bring forth flowers to surround us with beauty.
and let the mountains teach our hearts
to reach upward to heaven. Amen.

Daily Word, June 15, 2007
Every Cell of my body radiates pure life, energy and vitality.

I am a creation of divine life. Every strand of DNA in every cell of my body is lovingly designed and divinely formed.

As a beloved creation of God, I have a physical body that has an endless capacity to heal itself. Every cell is equipped with all that is necessary to restore perfect health.

Whether I am mending from a common cold or a major surgery, I know and affirm that a healing process is taking place. Divine intelligence is working through me now, establishing wholeness.

If a loved one or I have a medical procedure coming up, I trust God to work through the health care professionals to bring about the best outcome. Vibrant health is ours to claim. We are one with God, the source of pure life, energy and vitality.

"Daughter, your faith has made you well; go in peace, and be healed of your disease." Mark 5:34

Blessing Before Surgery
Out of the Ordinary, Joyce Rupp, *68.*

May the Divine Spirit give attentiveness and guidance to the surgical staff.

May you trust in your body's ability to heal.

May you have compassion for any part of your body that experiences pain or discomfort.

May you befriend your fears and be freed from all anxiety.

May you be at peace.

We send our love and our vitality to you. Receive this loving energy from our hearts to yours and be strengthened for your journey toward healing.

Jewish Prayer for the Body and for Healing:

Prayer for the body
Blessed are You, our Eternal God, Creator of the Universe, who has made our bodies in wisdom, creating openings, arteries, glands, and organs marvelous in structure, intricate in design. Should but one of them, by being blocked or opened, fail to function, it would be difficult to stand before You. Wondrous Fashioner and Sustainer of life, Source of our health and our strength, we give you thanks and praise.

Mi Sheberach
May the One who blessed our ancestors, Sarah and Abraham, Rebecca and Isaac, Leah, Rachel and Jacob bless *all those in the God Box* along with all of the ill among us. Grant insight to those who bring healing, courage and faith to those who are sick, love and strength to us and to all who love them. God, let your spirit rest upon all who are ill and comfort them. May they and we soon know a time of complete healing, a healing of the body and a healing of the spirit and let us say: Amen

Daily Word, October 15, 2007
As an expression of divine life, I radiate strength and vitality.

Focusing my mind on powerful, healing thoughts, I create a blessing of health for every one of the trillions of individual cells of my body. I state with firm intention: *As an expression of divine life, I radiate strength and vitality.* Every cell of my body receives this affirmation as a directive to express the wellness that is its natural state.

God's healing energy is moving in and through me now, and it is powerfully transformative. As I tap into this energy with my prayerful awareness, I am creating a healing vibration that moves through my body and out into my environment as words, attitudes and actions that support my well-being.

As an expression of divine life, I know that the strength and vitality that I am affirming is radiating throughout my body.

"Seek the One who is Life, your strength; walk harmoniously in Love's presence."
Psalm 105:4

Prayer for Healing

Belleruth Naparstek

Just give me this:
A rinsing out, a cleansing free of all my smaller
  strivings
So I can be the class act God intended,
True to my purpose,
All my energy aligned behind my deepest intention.

And just this:
A quieting down, a clearing away of internal ruckus,
So I can hear the huge stillness in my heart
And feel
How I pulse with all creation,
Part and parcel of Your great singing ocean.

And this, too:
A willingness to notice and forgive the myriad times
I fall short,
Forgetting who I really am,
What I really belong to.

So I can start over,
Fresh and clean
Like sweet sheets billowing in the summer sun,
My heart pierced with gratitude.

Hope and Trust

"Nothing will help us understand hope as much as a pilgrim's life, 'still and still moving,' day by day. And nothing will be as convincing to others as the way we exercise hope in our inner attitude and in our outward behavior . . .

"Hope does not even pretend that everything will be all right. Hope simply does its thing, like the spider in the corner of my bookshelf. She will make a new web again and again, as often as my feather duster swooshes it away—without self-pity, without self-congratulations, without expectations, without fear. If I could achieve the corresponding attitude on my level of consciousness, that would be hope alright."

—Gratefulness, the Heart of Prayer, David Steindl-Rast, 134–135

"Thus, every prayer of petition becomes a prayer of thanksgiving and praise as well, precisely because it is a prayer of hope. In the hopeful prayer of petition, we thank God for God's promise and we praise God for God's faithfulness.

"Our numerous requests simply become the concrete way of saying that we trust in the faithfulness of God's goodness Whenever we pray with hope, we put our lives in the hands of God. Fear and anxiety fade away and everything we are deprived of is nothing but a finger pointing out the direction of God's hidden promise which one day we shall taste in full."

—With Open Hands, Henri Nouwen, 73 .

"I need to stop. I need to stop and sip a cup of tea in the old wicker rocking chair out on our deck. I need days that are a sweet and slow ceremony, walking in these mountains where the very air has nourishment, walking as if I am a person free of regrets, free of worries about what might be . . . . The future exists only in our imaginations. It is a collective story waiting for our voices to express. That can only happen when you and I are willing to enter the emptiness, listening in the silence until we can understand how to create a future we can befriend . . . May we allow ourselves stillness so we can open our minds to ourselves, and

spaciousness so we can allow a moment of rest where all thoughts fly above
us like kites in a strong wind."

—*I Will Not Die and Unlived Life,*
Dawn Markova, 17-23 passim.

Psalm 20
Psalms for Praying, Nan Merrill, 33-34

May the One who created you in
                wholeness
    meet your needs when you call!
May the Name of Love be your
                protection
    and rise up in your heart as a
                tower of strength!
May all you have given in gratitude
                and with open hands
    be returned to you a hundredfold!
May your heart's desires and all
                your plans
    be fulfilled in due season!
Let us shout for joy as Love
                triumphs over fear;
Let our thankful hearts sing
    in loud acclamation to the
                Beloved,
    who answers our heartfelt
                prayers!
Now I know that Love comes to all
    who open their hearts, and
                dwells therein
    offering gifts of peace and
                harmony…
O Beloved, You who have created us,
                hear our call,
    make your home in our hearts!

The Lord Is My Pace-Setter, I shall Not Rush
Tokio Megashio, based on Psalm 23

He makes me stop and rest for quiet intervals,
He provides me with images of stillness,
which restore my serenity.
He leads me in ways of efficiency through calmness of mind,
And His guidance is peace.
Even though I have a great many things to accomplish each day,
I will not fret, for His presence is here.
His timelessness, His all-importance will keep me in balance,
He prepares refreshment and renewal in the midst of my activity.
By anointing my mind with His oils of tranquility,
My cup of joyous energy overflows.
Surely harmony and effectiveness shall be the fruit of my hours,
For I shall walk in the place of my Lord, and dwell in His house forever.
Amen.

From Psalm 27
Psalms for Praying, Nan Merrill, 46–47

"When fears assail me,
     rising up to accuse me,
Each one in turn shall be seen
     in Love's light.
Though a multitude of demons
     rise up within me
     my heart shall not fear....

One thing have I asked of Love,
     that I shall ever seek:
That I might dwell in the
          Heart of Love
     all the days of my life,
To behold the Beauty of my Beloved

and to know Love's plan.

For I shall hide in Love's heart
   in the day of trouble,
As in a tent in the desert,
Away from the noise of my fears.
And I shall rise above
   my struggles and pain,
Shouting blessings of gratitude
   in Love's Heart
And singing melodies of praise
   to my Beloved...

Do not turn away from me,
   You who have been my refuge.
Enfold me in your strong arms,
   O Blessed One.

Create in Me A Clean Heart,
Excerpt, based on Psalm 51:10, *Out of the Ordinary*, Joyce Rupp, 115

Create in me a clean heart, open and receptive, so that I may embrace the many ways you choose to visit my life.

Create in me a clean heart, purified through the daily disruptions and the life encounters that take me beyond my grasping control and ego-centeredness.

Create in me a clean heart, freed from the clutter of cultural enticements, so that I can enjoy the beauty of life's simple things and relish the gifts I easily take for granted.

Create in me a clean heart, brushed free of frantic busyness, so that I will have time to dwell with you in the listening space of solitude and silence.

Create in me a clean heart, cleansed of anxiety and lack of trust, restoring in me an enduring faith in your abiding presence and unconditional love.

From Psalm 68,
Psalms for Praying, Nan Merrill, 129-133 passim

Impregnate us with Love, O Comforter!
    Let our fears be transformed;
    let all that keeps us separated
    and confused flee!
As smoke is blown away, so let our
    fears rise up before You;
  as wax melts before the fire,
  let our fears be melted by Love!
    Then will we be released
            from bondage;
  we will exult before the Beloved;
  we will be jubilant with joy!...

O Beloved, reach into the hearts
    of your people,
  Enter into the darkness of
    their fears;
As the earth quakes, as floods strike
    without warning,
  let your Presence be near.
As the mountains tremble and volcanoes
    spew forth ash,
  let your Presence be near.
As rain falls in abundance on
    desert floors,
  restore the lands that they
    might flourish,
  that the flocks may roam and graze
    on fertile fields.

In your Mercy, O Beloved,
　　You provide for the needy,
　　　You are with us . . .

Yes, the Beloved will empower us
　　with love,
　　　as we face the fears within . . .

Call forth our strength, O Beloved;
　　stand by us as we break down
　　　the fears that bind us.
Because You dwell in our hearts,
　　we are strong and live
　　　with courage.

Let Nothing Disturb You , Teresa of Avila

Let nothing disturb you.
Let nothing frighten you.
All things pass.
God does not change.
Patience achieves everything.
Whoever has God lacks nothing.
God alone suffices.
Christ has no body on earth now but yours;
　　no hands but yours;
　　no feet but yours.
Yours are the eyes
　　through which the compassion of Christ
　　must look out on the world.
Yours are the feet
　　with which he is to go about doing good.
Yours are the hands
　　with which he is to bless his people.

Psalm 71
Psalms for Praying, Nan Merrill, 140–142

O Friend, be not far from me;
  O Beloved, come and enfold me
    in your Presence!
Help me to release my fears.
  Hear my prayer that they may be
    transformed,
O You, who are my Counselor.

As I surrender myself into your hands,
  I praise You more and more.
I tell others of your goodness,
  of your compassion and grace
    all the day;
  for your glory is beyond my
    understanding.
As I grow in inner peace and
    serenity,
  I sing songs of praise
    to You, my friend!

You who have done wondrous things,
  O Beloved, who is like You?
You who have seen me through
    many fears,
    strengthen me again;
From the depths of despair
    You renew my spirit,
You increase my trust, and You
    comfort me.

I praise you in the Silence
    of my heart,
    for your steadfast Love,

O my Beloved;
I offer prayers of gratitude,
O Holy One of the universe.
My heart leaps for joy, as
I whisper to You in
the night—
my soul also, which You
renew within me.
And I tell my friends as well as
strangers
of your abounding grace and
kindness.
For my fears have diminished,
my strength has returned;
I will live my remaining years
in peace.
Blessed be the Beloved, who dwells
in all hearts!

From *With Open Hands*
Henri Nouwen, 74

Dear God,
I am full of wishes,
full of desires,
full of expectations.
Some of them may be realized, many may not, but in the
midst of all my satisfactions and disappointments,
I hope in you.
I know that you will never leave me alone
and will fulfill your divine promises.
Even when it seems that things are not going my way,
I know that they are going your way
And that in the end your way is the best way for me.
O Lord, strengthen my hope,

especially when my many wishes are not fulfilled.
Let me never forget that your name is Love.

Psalm 137,
Psalms for Praying, Nan Merrill, 288

Plunge into the Ocean of Love,
    where heart meets Heart,
Where sorrows are comforted and
    wounds are mended.
There, melodies of sadness mingle with
    dolphin songs of joy;
Past fears dissolve in deep harmonic
      tones,
    the future—pure mystery.
For eternal moments lived in total
      Surrender
    glide smoothly over troubled waters.

Hide not from Love, O friends,
    sink not into the sea of despair,
      the mire of hatred.
Awaken, O my heart, that I drown not
      in fear!
Too long have I sailed where'ere
    the winds have blown!
      Drop anchor!
O Heart, of all hearts, set a
    clear course,
    that I might follow!
Guide me to the Promised Shore!

From *When Things Fall Apart*
Pema Chodron, 8

"When things are shaky and nothing is working, we might realize that we are on the verge of something. We might realize that this is a very vulnerable and tender place, and that tenderness can go either way. We can shut down and feel resentful or we can touch in on that throbbing quality. There is definitely something tender and throbbing about groundlessness."

Memorare
Remember, O most gracious Virgin Mary, that never was it known that anyone who fled to your protection, implored your help or sought your intercession was left unaided. Inspired with this confidence, I fly to you, O virgin of virgins, my Mother. To you I come, before you I stand, sinful and sorrowful. O Mother of the Word Incarnate, despise not my petitions, but in your mercy, hear and answer me. Amen.

From an Internet chain letter

May today be all you need it to be. May the peace of God and the freshness of the Holy Spirit rest in your thoughts, rule in your dreams tonight, and conquer all your fears. May God manifest God's self today in ways you have never experienced. May your joys be fulfilled, your dreams be closer, and your prayers be answered. I pray that faith enters a new height for you; I pray that your territory is enlarged. I pray for peace, healing, health, happiness, prosperity, joy, true and undying love for God.

I Am There
James Dillet Freeman

Do you need me? I am there.
You cannot see Me, yet I am the light you see by.
You cannot hear Me, yet I speak through your voice.
You cannot feel me, yet I m the power at work in your hands.

I am at work though you do not understand My ways.
I am at work though you do not recognize My works…

When you need Me, I am there.
Even if you deny Me, I am there.

Even when you feel most alone, I am there.
Even in your fears, I am there.
Even in your pain, I am there.
I am there when you pray and when you do not pray.

Though your faith in Me is unsure,
My faith in you never wavers,
because I know you, because I love you.

Beloved, I am there.

Leaning on the Heart of God
Out of the Ordinary, Joyce Rupp, 75.

Accept the strength that comes
from the grace of Christ Jesus
2 Timothy 2:1

I am leaning on the heart of God.
I am resting there in silence.
All the turmoil that exhausts me
is brought to bear on this great love.

No resistance or complaint is heard
as I lean upon God's welcome.
There is gladness for my coming.
There is comfort for my pain.

I lean, and lean, and lean
upon this heart that hurts with me.
Strength lifts the weight of my distress.
Courage wraps around my troubles.

No miracle of instant recovery.
No taking away life's burdens.
Yet, there is solace for my soul,
and refuge for my exiled tears.

It is enough for me to know
the heart of God is with me,
full of mercy and compassion,
tending to the wounds I bear.

The Hope of Loving
Meister Eckhart, *Love Poems from God,* translated by Daniel Ladinsky, 109

What keeps us alive, what allows us to endure?
        I think it is the hope of loving
                or being loved.

I heard a fable once about the sun going on a journey
        to find its source, and how the moon wept
                without her lover's
                    warm gaze.

We weep when light does not reach our hearts. We wither
        like fields if someone close
                does not rain their
                    kindness
                        upon
                        us.

From *The Last Lecture*
Randy Pausch, 111

"Leaving the doctor's office, I thought about what I said to Jai in the water park in the afterglow of the speed slide. 'Even if the scan results are bad tomorrow,' I had told her, 'I just want you to know that it feels great to be alive, and to be here today, alive with you. Whatever news we get about the scans, I'm not going to die when we hear it, I won't die the next day, or the day after that, or the day after that. So today, right now, well this is a wonderful day. And I want you to know how much I'm enjoying it.' I thought about that and about Jai's smile. I knew then. That's the way the rest of my life would need to be lived."

This Will Find You Ready
Judyth Hill

> *"Go I know not where,*
> *To get I know not what"*
> *Parsival, Wolfgang Von Escherbach*

When you lose everything, then you track.

This world is always spinning,
on chicken legs, at the edge of the forest.
You will need each chip of obsidian, every flake of flint,
all caught parts of conversations.

Glimpses of clematis behind fences in hidden courtyards.
To remember a soaker rain, trill of orioles at first light.

Every scent of hyacinth, of jasmine, is a vow,
every birdsong, the call to prayer,
a rooftop in another city, but always your own.

Call in all the magic.
Set a place at your table, silver knives, fishbones,
chess pieces of ancient ivory.

Can you see it? You've been so many times.

You've been the one who kneads the bread,
the one who comes to the table in sackcloth,
the one who sits beside the king, in aquamarine and emerald.
The crown, the crow, the crone.
It is all the same.

This time bring the sword,
This blade strikes once and once only.
Ask for leave, and do one thing right,
It's all you can do.
You must ask your question.

Permission will be given in both worlds.

There is a second chance,
at least in this story.

Tell it the old way, aloud.
Build a fire of the nine woods gathered, apple, hawthorn, hazel,
willow, rowan, vine and fir.

You already know. You have done this.

You will make what you desire appear, by your own seeking,
by your willingness
to sing as you approach,
to walk slowly, to keep going,

to serve what you walk towards with your whole,
broken,
wild heart.

In memory of Marie Hern ~ from her remembrance card:
May 29, 1927–April 29, 2008

Be Still and Know that I am God (Ps. 46:10)

I spoke to you …
before you were born, at your first thought,
   your first sight and your first word

Be still.
  Know that I am God.

      I speak to you…
through the clouds and rain, the splendor of the sun,
the waves of the sea and the peace of an evening

      Be still.
  Know that I am God.

    I will speak to you…
through the Wisdom of the Ancients,
at the end of time and throughout eternity

      Be still.
  Know that I am God.

Richard Rohr suggests we let go by breathing deeply, pausing between each line, saying:

   Be still and know that I am God.

    Be still and know that I am.

       Be still and know.

        Be still.

         Be

Love and Compassion

"Perhaps the most significant work that prayer does is to help us recognize the humility of other people and deepen our capacity for compassion and forgiveness. As we come to terms with our own limitations and our own need for kindness and understanding, we se more clearly the same need in others. Religious teaching may differ, but in the end we all live, suffer and die in much the same way, and we pray for the same things—peace, health, patience and forgiveness."

—*Talking to God*, John Gattuso, 12.

A Thought to begin your day . . .
Present Moment Wonderful Moment, Thich Nhat Hanh, 3

Waking up this morning, I smile.
Twenty-four brand new hours are before me.
I vow to live fully in each moment
And to look at all beings with eyes of compassion.

Prayer of Cardinal Newman

Dear Jesus, help us to spread your fragrance
everywhere we go.
Flood our souls with your spirit and life.
Penetrate and possess our whole being so utterly
that our lives may only be a radiance of yours.
Shine through us and be so in us
that every soul we come in contact with
may feel your presence in our soul.
Let them look up and see no longer us, but only Jesus.
Stay with us and then we shall begin to shine as you shine,
so to shine as to be light to others.
The light, O Jesus, will be all from you.
None of it will be ours.
It will be you shining on others through us.

Let us thus praise you in the way you love best
by shining on those around us.
Let us preach you without preaching,
not by words, but by our example;
by the catching force -
the sympathetic influence of what we do,
the evident fullness of the love our hearts bear to you.
Amen.

Daily Word, May 7, 2007
I am generous, peaceful, and compassionate.

My heart is a powerful center for receiving God's love and sharing this sacred expression of caring with others. With each realization of God's presence, I open myself to a fresh infilling of love.

From my heart of love, the qualities of generosity, peace and compassion flow out to others. As I think, speak, and act from the love in my heart, I connect with others at a deep spiritual level. I perceive the best in them and let them know how much joy their expressions of love bring to me.

Love is a sacred bond that all in the universal family of God share. Stronger than any challenge, more powerful than any misunderstanding, God's love unites all. We are one spirit, one heart.

"You shall love the Lord your God With all your heart, and with all your soul and with all your self . . . You shall love your neighbor as yourself." (Mt. 22:37–39)

What I Learned From My Mother
Sleeping Preacher, Julia Kasdorf

I learned from my mother how to love
the living, to have plenty of vases on hand
in case you have to rush to the hospital

with peonies cut from the lawn, black ants
still stuck to the buds. I learned to save jars
large enough to hold fruit salad for a whole
grieving household, to cube home-canned pears
and peaches, to slice through maroon grape skins
and flick out the sexual seeds with a knife point.
I learned to attend viewing even if I didn't know
the deceased, to press the moist hands
of the living, to look in their eyes and offer
sympathy, as though I understood loss even then.
I learned that whatever we say means nothing,
what anyone will remember is that we came.
I learned to believe I had the power to ease
awful pains materially like an angel.
Like a doctor, I learned to create
from another's suffering my own usefulness, and once
you know how to do this, you can never refuse.
To every house you enter, you must offer
healing: a chocolate cake you baked yourself,
the blessing of your voice, your chaste touch.

Love Does That

Meister Eckhart, *Love Poems from God,* translated by Daniel Ladinsky, 108

All Day long a little burro labors, sometimes
with heavy loads on her back and sometimes just with worries
about things that bother only
burros.

And worries, as we know, can be more exhausting
than physical labor.

Once in a while a kind monk comes
to her stable and brings
a pear, but more
than that,

he looks into the burro's eyes and touches her ears

and for a few seconds the burro is free
and even seems to laugh,

because love does
that.

Love frees.

"Capax Universi," Thomas Aquinas, *Love Poems from God*,
translated by Daniel Ladinsky, 134.

Capax universi, capable of the universe are your arms
when they move with love.

And I know it is true that your feet are never
more alive than when they are in
defense of a good
cause.

I want to fund your efforts: Stay near beauty, for she will always
strengthen you.

She will bring your mouth close to hers and
breathe—inspire you the way
light does the
fields.

The earth inhales God, why
should we not do
the same?

This sacred flame we tend inside needs
the chants of every tongue,
the communion with
all.

As capable as God
are we.

From *The Haunt of Grace: Responses to the Mystery of God's Presence*
Ted Loder, 101–108 passim

"When things get twisted out of shape for us, when pain hits, or loss, or failure, or illness, or the face in the mirror looks back with more sags and wrinkles than we remember gathering over the years, and the whole mysterious shebang of it overwhelms us with awe and questions we feel we're going to drown in, something in us whispers or screams out, 'Do you love me?' Do I matter, am I worth anything beyond this moment, or to those close beside me who matter so much to me.

"The incredible thing isn't just that our lives are twisted by wounds of one kind or another. The wonder is that there are those in our lives who kiss us anyway. It's a human kiss, but somehow more than that. Eternally more!

"Ornette Coleman once said that 'Jazz is the only music in which the same note can be played night after night but differently each time.' I think that's the one way jazz imitates God. Through lots of people—family, friends, even those we think of as enemies—God keeps twisting her or his lips to kiss our twisted lives so our lives not only still work . . . but still work gracefully. One note, grace, played differently in the lives of each of us. It gives us the pitch on which to start singing our song. It gives us a glimpse of who God is.

"Like jazz, it's enough. More than enough."

Instruments of God
May I Have This Dance?, Joyce Rupp, 117

A small, wooden flute,
an empty, hollow reed,
rests in her silent hand.

it waits the breath
of one who creates song
through its open form.

my often-empty life
rests in the hand of God;
like the hollowed flute,
it yearns for the melody
which only Breath can give.

the small, wooden flute and I,
we need the one who breathes,
we await one who makes melody.

and the one whose touch creates,
awaits our empty, ordinary forms,
so that the song-starved world
may be fed with golden melodies

In her reflection on this poem (123), Joyce writes:

"If there are days when we doubt our ability to be instruments of God's love, there are also times when we experience this truth very clearly. These are days when

- someone thanks us for something we've done that helped them significantly, even though we did not realize that we had done anything out of the ordinary

- we sense a deep harmony and oneness within for no particular reason

- we feel a strength within that we know is not ours alone

- we experience a bonding with the people with whom we live or work that goes beyond personalities and human perception

- we discover and claim a gift or an ability of ours because of its effect on others.

"I invite you to be an instrument of God's goodness. Develop your awareness each day of how God makes music through you. Discover anew how God's love touches others' lives because of your availability and openness to the divine musician's presence. Enjoy the song that God plays through you"

Celebration Prayer ~ Center for Ministry Development ~ 25 Years of Service

"There is always a moment in any kind of struggle when one feels in full-bloom. Vivid. Alive. One might be blown to bits in such a moment, and still be at peace . . . To be such a person or to witness anyone at this moment of transcendent presence is to know that what is human is linked, by a daring compassion, to what is divine.

"During my years of being close to people engaged in changing the world, I have seen fear turn into courage. Sorrow into joy. Funerals into celebrations. Because whatever the consequences, people, standing side by side, have expressed who they really are, and that ultimately they believe in the love of the world and each other."

—Alice Walker, *Anything We Love Can Be Saved*

And so we pray . . .
+ May God bless you with discomfort at easy
answers, half-truths, and superficial
relationships, so that you will live deep within
your heart.

+ May God bless you with anger at injustice,
    oppression, and using people and the earth so
    that you will work for justice, equity, and peace.

+ May God bless you with compassion for those
    who suffer because of others, and may you
    reach out to comfort them.

+ And may God bless you with the foolishness to
    think that you can make a difference where
    you are, in this world, in this ministry, in your
    surroundings, and that you can do the things
    which others say cannot be done.

+ We pray this, O God, in your name.
    Amen.

—Original author of prayer unknown, adapted by Alexis Navarro

The Love of God
Magdolene Mogyorosi

The love of God enfolds me
The love of God surrounds me
The love of God saturates me
The love of God upholds me
The love of God strengthens me
The love of God comforts me
The love of God cheers me
The love of God restores me
The love of God calms me
The love of God consoles me
The love of God guides me
The love of God protects me
The love of God cleanses me

The love of God frees me
The love of God fulfills me
The love of God heals me
The love of God uplifts me
The love of God embraces me
The love of God envelopes me
The love of God fills me
The love of God shines in me and eternally sustains me.

From *Creating True Peace*
Thich Nhat Hanh, 202

"Our practice everyday as bodhisattvas in training is to accept suffering and to learn to transform that suffering into hope, love, and compassion. We practice exactly like organic gardeners. They know that it is possible to transform garbage back into flowers. Let us learn to look at our suffering and the suffering of our world as a kind of compost. From that mud we can create the beautiful, fragrant lotuses of understanding and compassion. The flowers of understanding and compassion are already there in our hearts and minds in the form of seeds. Together we can practice to cultivate the flowers of understanding and compassion so that they can manifest every day for our happiness and well-being and the happiness and well-being of everyone around us."

Peace

A Chinese Proverb

If there is light in the soul,
There will be beauty in the person.
If there is beauty in the person,
There will be harmony in the house.
If there is harmony in the house,
There will be order in the nation.
If there is order in the nation,
There will be peace in the world.

Prayer for Peace
Mary Stewart

Keep us, O God
from all pettiness.
Let us be large in thought,
in word, in deed.
Let us be done
with fault-finding
and leave off all self-seeking.
May we put away all pretense
and meet each other face to face,
without self-pity
and without prejudice.
Grant that we may realize that
it is the little things of life
that create differences, that in the
big things of life we are as one
And, O God,
let us not forget to be kind.

Universal Peace Prayer

Lead me from death to life.
    from falsehood to truth.
Lead me from despair to hope,
    from fear to trust.
Lead me from hate to love,
    from war to peace,
Let peace fill my heart,
    my world, my universe.
    Amen.

A Buddhist Meditation

I am Peace, surrounded by Peace, secure in Peace.
Peace protects me
Peace supports me
Peace is in me
Peace is mine—All is well.
Peace to all beings
Peace among all beings
Peace from all beings
I am steeped in Peace, Absorbed in Peace, In the Streets, at our work,
having peaceful thoughts,
Peaceful words, peaceful acts.

WAGE PEACE
Judyth Hill, September 11, 2001

Wage peace with your breath.

Breathe in firemen and rubble,
        breathe out whole buildings and flocks of red wing
        blackbirds.

Breathe in terrorists
and breathe out sleeping children and freshly mown fields.

Breathe in confusion and breathe out maple trees.

Breathe in the fallen and breathe out lifelong friendships intact.

Wage peace with your listening: hearing sirens, pray loud.

Remember your tools: flower seeds, clothes pins, clean rivers.

Make soup.

Play music, memorize the words for thank you in three languages.

Learn to knit, and make a hat.

Think of chaos as dancing raspberries,
imagine grief
as the outbreath of beauty
or the gesture of fish.

Swim for the other side.

Wage peace.

Never has the world seemed so fresh and precious:

Have a cup of tea and rejoice.

Act as if armistice has already arrived.
Celebrate today.

Muslim, Jewish, Christian Prayer for Peace
Joan Chittister, OSB

O God, you are the source
of life and peace.
Praised be your name forever.
We know it is you who turn
our minds to thoughts of peace.
Hear our prayer in this time of war.

Your power changes hearts.
Muslims, Christians and Jews remember,
  and profoundly affirm,
that they are followers of the one God,
children of Abraham, brothers and sisters;
enemies begin to speak to one another;
those who were estranged
join hands in friendship; nations seek the way of peace together.

Strengthen our resolve to give witness
  to these truths by the way we live.
Give to us
Understanding that puts an end to strife;
Mercy that quenches hatred, and
Forgiveness that overcomes vengeance.
Empower all people to live in your law of love.   Amen.

The Prayer of St. Francis

Lord make me an instrument of your peace.
>Where there is hatred, let me sow love.
>Where there is injury, pardon.
>Where there is doubt, faith.
>Where there is despair, hope.
>Where there is darkness, light.
>Where there is sadness, joy.
O Divine Master, grant that I may not seek
>so much to be consoled as to console;
>to be understood, as to understand;
>to be loved, as to love;
>for it is in giving that we receive,
>it is in pardoning that we are pardoned,
>and in dying that we are born to eternal life.

Saint Theresa's Prayer
St. Theresa of Lisieux

May today there be peace within.
May you trust God that you are exactly
where you are meant to be.
May you not forget the infinite possibilities
that are born of faith.
May you use those gifts that you have received,
and pass on the love that has been given to you.
May you be content knowing you are a child of God.
Let this presence settle into your bones, and allow
your soul the freedom to sing, dance, praise and love.
It is there for each and every one of us.

Seasons

From "A New Year's Meditation,"
Out of the Ordinary, Joyce Rupp, 165

As you look back on the year just completed:

1. What name would you give to your journey of the past year?
    How would you describe it to one of your friends?
    What image or metaphor would you use to talk about it?

2. What were some of your "epiphanies" of this last year (your discoveries of the Holy One in your midst)?
    How did you grow because of them?

3. Who were your wise persons?
    What did they reveal to you?
    How did this influence your life?

From "February"
May I Have This Dance? Joyce Rupp, 36–39

(Context: Joyce begins with a little meditation on Ezekiel 37:14 in which she has you feel the bones in your body, being mindful of how you are created and shaped by your bones . . . to see their whiteness and their dryness. There is no life, no movement, only silence. Then she has you tell God about your dry bones . . . the situations where you lack life . . . how you feel about your deadness)

Listen to God speaking to you: "I am now going to make breath enter you and you will live . . . Hear God saying: "Come from the four winds, breath; breathe on these dry bones that they may come to life. Feel God's breath fill your dry bones . . ."

Then pray:

Response: Come from the four winds, breath; breathe on these dead, so that they may come to life. (Ez. 37:9)

We remember those who are deep in depression, whose inner world is bleak and dark . . .

We remember those who have recently said farewell to a loved one and who feel that joy will never return . . .

We remember those who are caught up in running through life and are entangled in frenzied activity . . .

We remember those who struggle to believe in their own goodness . . .

We remember those who have lost their dreams and their enthusiasm for life . . .

We remember those who are experiencing failure in relationships or in work situations . . .

We remember those who doubt their inner growth and who question their journey with God . . .

We remember those who never seem to get beyond financial worries and the pain of caring for the essentials of life . . .

We remember those who have been rejected, deserted, betrayed or abandoned . . .

We remember those who live in the grips of addiction and the throes of self-absorption . . .

We remember those who have lost hope and who daily do battle with thoughts of suicide . . .

We remember those who live constantly with worry and anxiety.

God, breath of life, there are moments when we feel like the dry bones filling Ezekiel's valley. When those times come upon us, help us to trust in you, to believe in your dance of life in us. Do not allow us to lose heart or to abandon hope. You can take the dry bones of our lives and enliven them in a way we have never dreamed possible. Bless our dry and dusty spirits with your deep and stirring love. Renew our dreams. Fill us with enthusiasm for life. May we always look to you as our source of life. Amen.

Lenten questions
May I Have This Dance? Joyce Rupp, 51

Will you believe that I love you without any reservations?
Will you trust me?
Will you let me be your strength?
Will you let go of your own strong control?
Will you believe in your own giftedness?
Will you walk with insecurity for a while?
Will you believe that I am inviting you to greater wholeness?
Will you allow my grace to move within you?
Will you open up your heart?
Will you come to me in prayer so I can empower you?
Will you drink of the living waters I bring to you?

From *May I Have This Dance?*
Joyce Rupp, 61–62

"Most of us are closed at one time or another. We all seek safety in certain areas of our lives. It is a natural, normal human response. In our desire for security, we sometimes fight the call to grow and to change. It takes trust to open up and to be receptive to Easter moments.

In our personal experiences of resurrection, there is the element of surrender and of great vulnerability. We are required to let go of our own agenda. We would like to plan this watering and refreshment of our souls ourselves. Just as we find the date for Easter on the calendar, we want to know when our hearts will be filled with joy again.

We also need to let go of our fearful questions: If I open up, will I be watered and nourished? Or will I be left open to dry out? Will I be barren and empty? Or will I be drenched and swallowed up by rains that never seem to stop? It can be difficult to let go of our insecurity. We are called to wait, to be open, expectant, and ready, believing with all our hearts that new growth will come.

We need to remember that God is with us, providing for us, watering our inner gardens. We will not be washed away nor will we be left dry forever. We simply must wait, in hope, with open minds and hearts. The rains will come and when they do, they will sing in our souls like an Easter alleluia.

As we enter into the resurrection stories let us hear God coaxing us to be open the way a welcome rainfall coaxes green out of a thirsty, dry garden. Let us hear God saying to us:

- open up your mind and your heart
- put aside your strong expectations
- lay down the arms of your inner violence
- give up your set ideas
- turn away from your winter worries
- let go of your oppressive fears
- be willing to be insecure for a while
- allow surprise to take over you heart.

Easter is about openness, about God coaxing growth from the turned over soil of our spirits. God waters the gardens of our hearts. Are we open and ready to receive the seeds of grace? Will the green shoot of divine life spring up in our inner garden?

Watered Gardens
May I Have This Dance?
Joyce Rupp, 55–56

God of little buds just now wearing green sleeves,
God of lilac limbs all full with signs of flowering,
God of fields plowed and black with turned-over earth,
God of screeching baby bird mouths widely awaiting food,

God of openness, of life and of resurrection,
Come into this Easter season and bless me.
Look around the tight, dead spaces of my heart
That still refuse to give you an entrance.

Bring your gentle but firm love.
Begin to lift the layers of resistance
That hang on tightly deep inside of me.

Open, one by one, those places in my life
Where I refuse to be overcome by surprise.
Open, one by one, those parts of my heart
Where I fight the entrance of real growth.
Open, one by one, those aspects of my spirit
Where my security struggles with the truth.

Keep me open to the different and the strange;
Help me to accept the unusual and also the ordinary;
Never allow me to tread on others' dreams
By shutting them out, closing them up,
By turning them off or pushing them away.

God of the Resurrection, God of the living,
Untomb and uncover all that needs to live in me.
Take me to people, events, and situations
And stretch me into much greater openness.

Open me. Open me. Open me.
For it is only then that I will grow and change.
For it is only then that I will know how it is
To be in the moment of rising from the dead.

You will be like a watered garden,
like a flowing spring
whose waters never run dry. Isaiah 58:11

"The Easter Challenge"
Out of the Ordinary, Joyce Rupp, 87.

You believe because you can see . . .
Happy are those who have not seen
and yet believe.
                    –John 20:29
Every year it happens:
earth shakes her sleepy head,
still a bit wintered and dull,
and feels new life stirring

Every year cocoons give up their treasures,
fresh shoots push through brown leaves,
seemingly dead branches shine with green,
and singing birds find their way home

Every year we hear the stories

empty tomb, surprised grievers,
runners with news and revelation,
unexpected encounters,
conversations on the road,
tales of nets filling with fish,
and breakfast on a seashore

And every year
the dull and dead in us
meets our Easter challenge:

to be open to the unexpected,
to believe beyond our security,
to welcome God in every form,
and trust in our own greening

Easter: The Resurrection of the Lord, from *Lent: Sunday Readings*
Megan McKenna, 197

"The good news goes first to his brothers and friends. His sisters carry it forth and were told not to be afraid—of anything or anyone! They are to go with peace. Peace is the undeniable presence of the Risen Lord. Peace, not as the world gives, but peace that knows what sin and evil can do, the scars it leaves behind, but also knows the life that is unquenchable within and the Spirit that is irrepressible and indestructible.

"This story is ours, too. Peace to all of us who have come seeking the crucified One, now risen in glory. We bend and embrace his feet and do him homage. Then we run into the world and spread the good news to our friends, to whom we are bound in baptism and the Spirit. Then we go out into the wider world, to our Galilee, our cities and outskirts of the realms of power, and seek him there. We find him where he is most at home—among the poor and those who struggle for dignity and a life that death cannot tear apart.

"Today we proclaim that we believe in the resurrection. What is resurrection? In *Blessed Are You Who Believe*, Carlo Carretto describes resurrection this way:

"When the world seems a defeat for God and you are sick with the disorder, the violence, the terror, the war on the streets, when the earth seems to be chaos, say to yourself," Jesus died and rose again on purpose to save, and his salvation is already with us.

"When your father or your mother, your son or your daughter, your spouse or your friend are on their deathbed, and you are looking at them in the pain of parting, say, 'We shall see each other again in the Kingdom; courage.'

Every departing missionary is an act of faith in the resurrection.
Every newly-opened leper hospital is an act of faith in the resurrection.
Every peace treaty is an act of faith in the resurrection.
Every agreed commitment is an act of faith in the resurrection.
When you forgive your enemy
When you feed the hungry
When you defend the weak you believe in the resurrection.
When you have the courage to marry
When you welcome the newly born child
When you build your home you believe in the resurrection.
When you wake at peace in the morning
When you sing to the rising sun
When you go to work with joy you believe in the resurrection."

Psalm to Virgin Spring,
Prayers for a Planetary Pilgrim, Edward Hays, 108

Drawn upward by some hidden power,
   life is crackling the crust of earth
   and bursting forth from limb and stem.
Your aroma, O Life-giver,
   is upon the springtime wind,
   and I feel its power
   stirring deep within me.

Green is your color, O God,
   the green of new life
   that lovingly transfigures earth's dreariness,

long held prisoner
by the icy web of winter's cold.

Green up my heart with hope,
   in your perpetual promise of life.
Send forth from my soul
   new shoots, fresh buds
   eager to grow in your divine image.

May this year's visit of virgin Spring
   make my heart a virgin once again
   intoxicated with wild love for you,
   whom I discover in all things
   and in everyone.

Awaken Me
Out of the Ordinary, Joyce Rupp, 82

Risen One,
come meet me
in the garden of my life.

Lure me into elation.
Revive my silent hope.
Coax my dormant dreams.
Raise up my neglected gratitude.
Entice my tired enthusiasm.
Give life to my faltering relationships.
Roll back the stone of my indifference.
Unwrap the deadness in my spiritual life.
Impart heartiness in my work.

Risen One,
send me forth as a disciple of your unwavering love,
a messenger

of your unlimited joy.

Resurrected One,
may I become
ever more convinced
that your presence lives on,
and on, and on
and on.

Awaken me!
Awaken me!

Let Me Live Grace-fully,
Guerrillas of Grace, Ted Loder, 125
Thank you, Lord,
for this season
   of sun and slow motion,
      of games and porch sitting,
         of picnics and light green fireflies
            on heavy purple evenings;
and praise for slight breezes.
It's good, God,
as the first long days of your creation.

Let this season be for me
   a time of gathering together the pieces
      into which my busyness has broken me.
O God, enable me now
   to grow wise through reflection,
      peaceful through the song of the cricket,
         recreated through the laughter of play.

Most of all Lord,
let me live easily and grace-fully for a spell,
   so that I may see other souls deeply,

share in a silence unhurried,
   listen to the sound of sunlight and shadows,
      explore barefoot the land of forgotten dreams and shy hopes
         and find the right words to tell another who I am.

A Labor Day Reflection:

What is your work doing for you?
What is your work doing to you?
Are you happy with the kind of person you're becoming through your work?
How can you find God in your work situation?

Prayer for Autumn Days,

May I Have This Dance? Joyce Rupp, 139

God of the seasons, there is a time for everything; there is a time for dying and a time for rising. We need courage to enter into the transformation process.

God of autumn, the trees are saying goodbye to their green, letting go of what has been. We, too, have our moments of surrender, with all their insecurity and risk. Help us to let go when we need to do so.

God of fallen leaves lying in colored patterns on the ground, our lives have their own patterns. As we see the patterns of our own growth, may we learn from them.

God of misty days and harvest moon nights, there is always the dimension of mystery and wonder in our lives. We always need to recognize your power-filled presence. May we gain strength from this.

God of harvest wagons and fields of ripened grain, many gifts of growth lie within the season of our surrender. We must wait for harvest in faith and hope. Grant us patience when we do not see the blessings.

God of geese going south for another season, your wisdom enables us to know what needs to be left behind and what needs to be carried into the future. We yearn for insight and vision.

God of flowers touched with frost and windows wearing white designs, may your love keep our hearts from growing cold in the empty seasons.

God of life, you believe in us, you enrich us, you entrust us with the freedom to choose life. For this we are grateful.

The Falling Leaves
May I Have This Dance? Joyce Rupp, 129–130

with a constant chorus of cicadas
the leaves tumble down,
from long, thin silver poplars,
they twirl to the ground,
dancing the Autumn death dance
beneath the great blue sky.

the leaves seem glad at the going.
(is there something I don't know?)
sparkling in the October sunshine,
they fill the air with gentle rustling.

one, then another and another,
on they skim down from above,
bedding the forest table before me
with comforting crunches and crackles.

this gigantic death scene of leaves
does not smell of sorrow and sadness,
rather, the earth is colored with joy
and the leaves make music in the wind.

why is this dance of death so lovely?
why do leaves seem so willing to go?
are they whispering to each other,
urging one another to be freed?

maybe "you first and then I'll follow"
or: "'you can do it, go ahead"
supporting one another gladly
in their call to final surrender.

I have not yet discovered the secret
of the serenity of sailing leaves;
every autumn I walk among them
with a longing that stretches forever,
wanting to face that death-dance
and the truth of my own mortality.

"Like clothes, every body will wear out,
The age-old law is, 'Everyone must die.'
Like foliage growing on a bushy tree,
some leaves falling, others growing,
so are the generations of flesh and blood:
one dies, another is born." --Sirach 14:18-20'

Waken in Me a Sense of Joy
Guerrillas of Grace, Ted Loder, *126*
O extravagant God,
in this ripening, red-tinged autumn,
waken in me a sense of joy
            in just being alive.
joy for nothing in general
   except for everything in particular;
joy in sun and rain
   mating with the earth to birth a harvest;
joy in soft light

through shyly disrobing trees;
joy in acolyte moon
   setting halos around processing clouds;
joy in the beating of a thousand wings
   mysteriously knowing which way is warm;
joy in wagging tails and kids' smiles
   and in this spunky old city;
joy in the taste of bread and wine
   the smell of dawn,
       a touch,
          a song,
             a presence;
joy in having what I cannot live without—
   other people to hold and cry and laugh with;
joy in love,
   in you;
and that all at first and last
is grace.

"I Am Silent . . . and Expectant" *(Advent)*
Guerrillas of Grace, Ted Loder , *132*

How silently,
How silently
The wondrous gift is given.

I would be silent now,
Lord,
and expectant…
      that I may receive
         the gift I need
            so I may become
               the gift others need.

Sharon's Christmas Prayer
The Hour of the Unexpected, John Shea

She was five,
   sure of the facts,
   and recited them
   with slow solemnity,
   convinced every word
   was revelation.
   She said
The were so poor
they had only peanut butter and jelly sandwiches
to eat
and they went a long way from home
without getting lost. The lady rode
a donkey, the man walked, and the baby
was inside the lady.
They had to stay in a stable
with an ox and an ass (tee hee)
but the Three Rich Men found them
because a star lited the roof.
Shepherds came and you could
pet the sheep but not feed them.
Then the baby was borned.
And do you know who he was?

Her quarter eyes inflated
   to silver dollars,
The baby was God.

   And she jumped in the air
   whirled round, dove into the sofa
   and buried her head under the cushion
   which is the only proper response
   to the Good News of the Incarnation.

Suffering and Death

"Eternity is born in time, and everytime someone dies whom we have loved dearly, eternity can break into our mortal existence a little bit more."—

—Henri Nouwen

"When we live in communion with God, when we belong to God's own household, there is no longer any 'before" or "after.' Death is no longer the dividing line. Death has lost its power over those who belong to God, because God is the God of the living, not of the dead. Once we have tasted the joy and peace that come from being embraced by God's love, we know that all is well and will be well. 'Don't be afraid,' Jesus says. 'I have overcome the powers of death . . . come and dwell with me and know that where I am your God is.'"

—"Death No Longer the Dividing Line," *Here and Now,*
Henri Nouwen

"God has sent people to be very close to you as you gradually let go of the word that holds you captive. You must trust fully in their love. Then you will never feel completely alone. Even though no one can do it for you, you can make the lonely passage in the knowledge that you are surrounded by a safe love and that those who let you move away from them will be there to welcome you on the other side. The more you trust in the love of those God has sent to you, the more you will be able to lose your life and so gain it.

"Success, notoriety, affection, future plans, entertainment, satisfying work, health, intellectual stimulation, emotional support—yes even spiritual progress—none of these can be clung to as if they are essential for survival. Only as you let go of them can you discover the true freedom your heart most desires. That is dying, moving into the life beyond life. You must make that passage now, not just at the end of your earthly life. You cannot do it alone, but with the love of those who are being sent to you, you can surrender your fear and let yourself be guided into the new land."

—"Let Others Help You Die," *The Inner Voice of Love,*
Henri Nouwen.

"There is no one who does not have to choose sometime, someway, between giving up and growing stronger as they go along. And yet, if we give up in the midst of struggle, we never find out what the struggle would have given us in the end. If we decide to endure it to the end, we come out changed by the doing of it. It is a risk of mammoth proportions. We dare the development of the self."

—*Scarred by Struggle, Transformed by Hope,*
Joan Chittister, OSB, 2.

DEATH
(for one who is dying)
Suzette Haden Elgin

I go from you
into a new becoming;
rejoice for me and wish me an easy journey
into the Light.
The winds will speak to you of me,
the waters will mention my name;
snow and rain and fog,
first light and last light,
all will remind you that I had
a certain way of being
that was dear to you.
I go back to the land I came from
and on beyond.
Watch for me,
from Time to Time.
Amen.

DEATH
(for one who has died)
Suzette Haden Elgin

You go from us
into a new becoming;
we rejoice for you and wish you an easy journey
into the Light.
The winds will speak to us of you,
the waters will mention your name;
snow and rain and fog,
first light and last light,
all will remind us that you had
a certain way of being
that was dear to us.
You go back to the land you came from
and on beyond.
We will watch for you,
from Time to Time.
Amen.

Morning Prayer to the Angel of Death,
Prayers for the Domestic Church, Edward Hays, 179

Come Death,
 and be my counselor, my personal advisor,
 as I meet the numerous challenges of my day.
The great and powerful are surrounded by their advisors
 who assist them in making important decisions,
 but I am a simple person without such wise counselors.
Yet, I, even as a simpler person,
 must make choices and decisions
that will determine the course of my life
and even of the lives of others.
I, too, need guidance and wisdom.

So come Death,
> be near and shadow my day,
> and pass your gray shadow
over the choices that I consider.
Remind me, O Friend and Constant Companion,
> that life is indeed brief
> and that today and its joys are fleeting
> and may never come my way again.
Nudge me with your boney finger, O Death,
> and remind me that the only truly important things in life
are my relationships
with God, with those I love, and with myself.
Show to me, Dark Friend of the Underworld,
> that balance sheet which proves
> that those things we think important
> are seldom truly of importance,
> and those things we may think not important
> are truly the telling things of our short, short lives.
Counsel me, Teacher of the Tombs,
> that time taken to drink-in a sunset,
> to marvel at the butterfly upon the leaf
> or the faces of children at play —
> that these time and others like them
> are more valuable than gold or the most precious of jewels.
Come, Angel of Death,
> and guide, this day, my choices in life.

Amen

From: *Way of the Cross: Gateway to Resurrection*
Joan Chittister, 28–33.

XII: Jesus dies on the cross: The 12th station of the cross brings us face-to-face with the finality of defeat. Sometimes things don't have a happy ending in life. Sometimes we fail. Sometimes we're beaten. Sometimes we're lost.

Sometimes we're humiliated. Sometimes we're misunderstood. Sometimes we are abandoned by the very people we love most in life and whom we thought also loved us. At that point, without doubt, something in us dies. There's no going back to things as they were before. Then doors close in our hearts and the old breath goes out of us and all we can do is surrender to the dark. It is not a pretty moment. It can take all the energy we have. **The question** with which the 12th station confronts us is an awesome one: Am I able to accept the daily deaths of life, both the great ones and the small, knowing that death is not the end of life, only its passing over to something new in me? Hopefully, I learn from Jesus who gave up himself, his mission, his life in ways that all seem totally wrong, that the deaths I die may bring new life to the world around me as well. *Prayer: Jesus, at this moment I do accept from your hands whatsoever deaths you shall choose to send me this day, with all their pains and griefs.*

XIII: Jesus is taken down from the cross. The 13th station of the cross with its spectre of irrevocable loss, its futile efforts, its wasted dreams, drains the human soul to the point of numbness. Can anything worse be imagined than the death of the ideal? When Jesus is taken down from the cross, when hope dies, when everything we ever wanted gets thrown away, discarded, overlooked, ignored, forgotten, we eat the dust of despair. We wonder what life was ever about if this is all it comes to—despite all the good will, all our great struggles to have it be otherwise. Then, we realize that only God is God, that we are not in charge of time or truth or the perfect world. Then, we give ourselves over to the arms of God and trust. **The question** on which the 13th station concentrates us is a straightforward one: Am I prepared to let go of everything I ever wanted so God's will can come another way?

Prayer: Jesus, when I am tempted to insist on being able to control the situations of my life beyond your other ways of breaking me open to new ideas, new insights, new beginnings, give me the grace in the midst of my pain to let go.

XIV: Jesus is laid in the tomb. The 14th station of the cross brings us to grapple with the grace of closure. Some phases of life end and cannot be retrieved. They go by before we're ready to see them go. Worse, their going may feel like ignominy at the time or may even look to the world like failure. It may sting with grave injustice and may grieve us beyond all telling of it. But only in the ability to realize that life goes on from one stage to another, from one moment to another, from one task to another, from one kind of presence to another can we ever come to new life. When Jesus submits to the death of his ministry, when Jesus allows both state and synagogue to cast him out, one life ends so that another one can begin. **The question** which the 14th station of the cross leaves in our soul is a resounding one: Am I able to trust that the tombs of my life are all gateways to resurrection?

Prayer: Jesus, give me the grace to see in all the dead ends of my life an invitation to new life.

Thich Nhat Hanh — Oct. 2, 07 Notes from his presentation at USD
TNH talked quite a bit about suffering (the central teaching in Buddhism . . . all life suffers) . . . and talked about embracing it like you would a little baby that is crying or needing attention . . . to hold it, caress it, be kind to it . . . and then learn what it needs. He said the greatest learning comes from our suffering. No mud, no lotus, is the way he expressed it. When you look at a flower, think about the mud it grew out of. When you see the mud, see the flower, when you see the flower, remember the mud!

Pema Chodron
When Things Fall Apart, 8

"Things falling apart is a kind of testing and also a kind of healing . . . The healing comes from letting there be room for all of this to happen: room for grief, for relief, for misery, for joy . . . Letting there be room for not knowing is the most important thing of all . . . When there's a big disappointment, we don't know if that's the end of the story. It may be just the beginning of a great adventure."

A Prayer for Those who Wake or Watch or Weep Tonight
St. Augustine

Watch now, dear Lord,
with those who wake or watch or weep tonight,

and give your angels charge over those who sleep.
Tend your sick ones, rest your weary ones,
bless your dying ones, soothe your suffering ones,
pity your afflicted ones, shield your joyous ones,
and all for your love's sake.
Amen.

Coming or Going
Dogen.

The migrating bird leaves
no trace behind
and does not need a guide.

Miscellaneous

From *In Search of Belief, 3*
Joan Chittister, OSB

"One of Hinduism's holy books, the Mahabharata, celebrates what Hindus call 'The Thousand Names of Vishnu.' Among the names of God, the Mahabharata says, are the Creator, Giver of Peace, the All-Knowing, the Inexhaustible Treasure, Being, the Uplifter, Jasmine, Water Lily, Lover of Devotees, Patience, the Supreme Self, Sustainer of Life, Stealer of Hearts, Answerer of Prayers, Maker and Destroyer of Fear, Holder of the Wheel of the Cosmos, Protector, Who Enjoys the Nectar of Immortality. It is a panoply of everything the mystics of that tradition name as part and parcel of the Godhead. It is a plethora of qualities, of insights, of awarenesses about the all-encompassing nature of God. It is the kind of contemplation designed to break open the soul, to stretch it beyond itself, to make earth the stuff of which heaven is made. It is a demonstration of contemplative consciousness. It is also sound theology and good spirituality."

From *Everyday Simplicity*
Robert Wicks, 69

"Meditate on how planning and preparing have resulted in your missing so much of life. Do this until you become so disgusted that you vow to plan 5% and live, fully live, the other 95%. Also seek to make all things new by having a willingness to "unlearn." Be open to new knowledge rather than being captured by old teachings and experiences."

A Psalm Before Beginning Work
Prayers for a Planetary Pilgrim, Edward Hays, 188

To you O Divine One, from whose hands
    comes the work of creation, so artfully designed,

I pray that this work I am about to do
may be done in companionship with you.
May the work that I will soon begin
sing praise to you
as songbirds do.
May the work that I will soon begin
add to the light of your presence
because it is done with great love.
May the work that I will soon begin
speak like a prophet of old
of your dream of beauty and unity.
May the work that I will soon begin
be a shimmering mirror of your handiwork
in the excellence of its execution,
in the joy of doing it for its own sake,
in my poverty of ownership over it,
in my openness to failure or success,
in my invitation to others to share in it
and in its bearing fruit for the world.
May I be aware that through this work
I draw near to you.
I come to you, Beloved.

Five Finger Prayer
Paul Ciniraj, Kerala, India

1. Your thumb is nearest you. So begin your prayers by praying for those closest to you. They are the easiest to remember. To pray for our loved ones is, as C. S. Lewis once said, a "sweet duty."
2. The next finger is the pointing finger. Pray for those who teach, instruct and heal. This includes teachers, doctors, and ministers. They need support and wisdom in pointing others in the right direction. Keep them in your prayers.
3. The next finger is the tallest finger. It reminds us of our leaders. Pray for the president, leaders in business and industry, and administrators.

These people shape our nation and guide public opinion. They need God's guidance.

4. The fourth finger is our ring finger. Surprising to many is the fact that this is our weakest finger; as any piano teacher will testify. It should remind us to pray for those who are weak, in trouble or in pain. They need your prayers day and night. You cannot pray too much for them.

5. And lastly comes our little finger; the smallest finger of all which is where we should place ourselves in relation to God and others. As the Bible says, "The least shall be the greatest among you." Your pinkie should remind you to pray for yourself. By the time you have prayed for the other four groups, your own needs will be put into proper perspective and you will be able to pray for yourself more effectively.

"A Prayer to Be Freed from the Tizzies"[32]
Out of the Ordinary, Joyce Rupp, *65.*

Dear God,
You who did not invent tizzies,
be with me when I get caught
in the wild worrying of my mind,
and the needless scurrying around
in my fearful heart.

Trip me up when I fret and stew
so I can see the trap of tizzies,
with their schemes to keep me
bunched up in stress and strain.

Let me fall headfirst into the truth
of your never-ending presence,
wrap your kind arms around me
and calm my doubts and fears.

Shout loudly in my spiritual ear
when my nerves get knotted,
my mind feels cramped,
and my stomach screams.

It may be difficult,
but do try to get my full attention,
because tizzies are not healthy,
and they definitely chase peace
out the front door of my heart.

Dear God, you did not invent tizzies,
I did,
and only I can send them on their way,
and I will,
if you strengthen me
to let go of my anxious hold.

A process for dealing with hardship
from *www.gratefulness.org*

Think of hardship as an invitation. Any difficulty you encounter can draw out the highest good in you.

1. Name one personal quality you'll most need to meet the difficulty (e.g., flexibility, patience, hope, humor, kindheartedness, devotion, simplicity, strength, humility, discernment, truth-telling, sensitivity, forgiveness, confidence).
2. What quality does this obstacle call me to develop?
3. Call upon your chosen quality. Repeat it. Symbolize it. Draw on it like buckets from a well, as if it's already there.

Even in extreme circumstances, all things work for good.

The Our Father: (A Paraphrase)

From Many, One, Edward Francis Gabriele, 122

Tender God,
Who lives in heaven and earth,
In human reason and passion,
you are the Holy One in our midst.
Your justice is our peace;
your peace is our hope;
your presence, our delight!
Make our hands, your hands;
Our hearts, your heart;
Our lives, your life!
Give us this day and always
a bread of freedom to share,
a cup of hope to pour upon the earth.
Forgive us our hatreds and walls.
Teach us to forgive the walls of others as well.
Do not permit us tests beyond our strength.
And deliver us from Evil's death-grip.
For everything above us and under us,
everything within us and without us,
must bend the knee
to the Glory of your Freedom,
the everlasting Victory
of your Justice and Peace!

Sources of Wisdom in the God Box

Welcome to my library! Here are the resources I dip into frequently as I attempt to develop my own spiritual life. These are the books from which many prayers in *The God Box* come.

Borysenko, Joan. Pocketful of Miracles. New York: Warner Books, 1994.

Chittister, Joan. *In Search of Belief.* Ligouri, Missouri: Ligouri Press, 1999.

————. *Scarred by Struggle; Transformed by Hope.* Grand Rapids: Wm. B. Eerdsman Publishing Co., 2005.

————. *Way of the Cross: Gateway to Resurrection.* Erie: Benetvision, 1999.

Chodron, Pema. *When Things Fall Apart.* Boston: Shambala Press, 1997.

Cummings, E. E. *100 Selected Poems.* New York: Grove Press. 1954.

Daily Word. Unity Village, Missouri: Unity School of Christianity.

Dear, John. *The Advent of the God of Peace.* Erie: Pax Christi USA, 2007.

Durback, Robert. *Seeds of Hope: A Henri Nouwen Reader.* New York: An Image Book, Doubleday, 1989, 1997.

Gabriele, Edward Francis. *From Many, One.* Notre Dame: Ave Maria Press, 1995.

Gattuso, John, ed. *Talking to God.* Milford, New Jersey: Stone Creek Publications, 2006.

Gilbert, Elizabeth. *Eat, Pray, Love.* New York: Penguin, 2006.

Hanh, Thich Nhat. *Creating True Peace.* New York: Free Press, 2003.

Hays, Edward. *Prayers for the Planetary Pilgrim.* Notre Dame: Forest of Peace, Ave Maria Press, 1989, 2008.

———. *Prayers for the Domestic Church.* Notre Dame: Forest of Peace, Ave Maria Press, 1979, 2007.

Keillor, Garrison. *Good Poems for Hard Times.* New York: Penguin, 2005.

Ladinsky, Daniel, transl. *Love Poems from God.* New York: Penguin, 2002.

Kozak, Pat and Janet Schaffran. *More Than Words: Prayer and Ritual for Inclusive Communities.* Oak Park, Illinois: Meyer Stone Books, 1988.

Loder, Ted. *Guerrillas of Grace.* Philadelphia: Innisfree Press, 1984.

———. *My Heart in my Mouth.* Philadelphia: Innisfree Press, 2000.

———. *The Haunt of Grace.* Philadelphia: Innisfree Press, 2002.

Markova, Dawna. *I Will Not Die an Unlived Life.* York Beach: Red Wheel/Weiser, 2000.

McKenna, Megan. *Lent: The Sunday Readings.* Dublin: Veritas, 2008

Merrill, Nan. *Psalms for Praying.* New York: Continuum, 1996.

Nouwen, Henri. *With Open Hands.* Notre Dame: Ave Maria Press, 1972.

Pausch, Randy. *The Last Lecture.* New York: Hyperion. 2008.

Rolheiser, Ron. *Daybreaks: Reflections for Lent and Easter,* Ligouri, Missouri: Ligouri, 2005.

Rupp, Joyce. *May I Have This Dance?* Notre Dame: Ave Maria Press, 1992.

———. *Out of the Ordinary.* Notre Dame: Ave Maria Press, 3rd ed., 2000.

Shannon, Maggie Oman. *The Way We Pray: Celebrating Spirit from Around the World.* Berkeley: Conari Press, 2001.

———. *Prayers for Healing.* Berkeley: Conari Press, 1997.

———. *Prayers for Hope and Comfort.* San Francisco: Conari Press, 2008.

Shea, John. *An Experience Named Spirit.* Chicago: Thomas More Association, 1983.

Steindl-Rast, David. *Gratefulness, the Heart of Prayer.* Ramsey: Paulist Press, 1984.

Wicks, Robert. *Everyday Simplicity.* Notre Dame: Sorin Books, 2000.

Wiederkehr, Macrina. *Seven Sacred Pauses.* Notre Dame: Sorin Books, 2008.

Afterword

Hee-haw for Health

I love a picture my friend Lynn sent: bald-
headed with thumbs and fingers become antlers
sticking out from both sides of her face waving for a
charge, laughing at the absurdity of life without belief . . .

The photo hung for the longest time on our
bathroom mirror where it greeted us every day
as we faced another day seeing what the world sees
when we walk out the door, without a clue what's inside . . .

I take strength from Lynn's grin, her "hee-haw
for health" because it comes not from her despair
but from her trust that medicine having done its best
she can rest faith in God and "give the raspberries" to fear . . .

Or since, as theologian-poet Karen Armstrong says:
"There is nothing human beings can do to think Being
into existence," the fact that we show up existing gives us
ample reason to celebrate that all of being, life, is from God . . .

and is perfect once we see as we are seen.

-dr
-for Lynn Neu, no longer bald, 3-1-2005
*Karen Armstrong: *A History of God*
 New York: Alfred A. Kopf, 1994, p. 388.

Appendix A:

Seasons of Life in the God Box

To everything there is a season—a time to be born, a time to die; a time to laugh, a time to mourn; a time of war, a time of peace. As I begin each week's God Box, I'm forced take a deep breath and look back. What time is it? What happened this week? What happened to me? To the ones I love? To the world around me and a world away? What grabbed my attention? What may have grabbed theirs?

In these letters that open up the Box each week, the seasons of life play out. Here you will witness seasons of joy and celebration, sickness and death, hope and fear. You will meet inspiring people, suffering people, faithful people. You will bump into new life and eternal life. From fires and disaster to falling leaves and ocean breezes, life weaves a tapestry, and we are somehow woven into it.

April 3, 2006
Here I am . . . asking for prayers for myself again as we continue to explore what the docs are seeing on 2 mammograms and an ultrasound. Something is there, but they can't really tell what it is. It's small, but seems to have an "echo" or slight shadow. I will have a needle biopsy on Thursday (results 3 days after) to determine if it's cancer. The doctor said it was not an emergency for me to get in for the biopsy . . . and that it may be nothing. Even if it is "something," it

sounds like it would be dealt with quite easily. My hope is that with all your love and prayers, they'll be surprised to see nothing there, scratch their heads and wonder where it went! It's not impossible, you know!

At the risk of rambling on . . . when I told the doctor that somehow after going through ovarian cancer, I don't feel panic, she said that though she didn't know what my experience was like, she'd been hit by a train once herself. I thought she meant that figuratively, but as I looked again at her shirt sleeve hanging loosely at her side, empty, I asked if she'd lost her arm that way. Standing there, she said "Yes, and I lost both legs as well!" I was dumbstruck! Then she went on . . . "you know once you have something like this, you just hear what you have to do and start working the plan. And the very exciting thing is that even after losing both legs and my arm, I got married and I have two lovely children!" Her presence was sheer joy . . . and hope and careful care. I feel confident that if something is there, she will find it! And, we'll deal with it . . . one step at a time.

August 28, 2006
Good *Tuesday* Morning All!

This has been quite a week . . . mixed with lots of family fun and the death of our dear friend Tom. We've been praying for him for some time as he struggled with anorexia. He seemed to be bouncing back on Friday morning, but at about 3:30 p.m., he took a turn for the worse and began his journey home. When nothing more could be done, "comfort care" was ordered. This meant that Tom's by-pap oxygen mask would be removed and life would take its natural course. Tom died in his wife Paula's arms on Saturday morning at 4:40 a.m.

Amazingly, just after the mask was removed and morphine delivered, he "came to." His eyes opened and he began to pray along with us as we fell back upon those old familiar, comfortable prayers . . . Our Father . . . Hail Mary . . . Glory be . . . . We fumbled to sing something we all knew . . . Amazing Grace. Tom mouthed the words with us. Kisses for Paula, phone calls from family, time to reminisce, laughter, tears, time to say good-bye.

It was all so difficult and so beautiful. Again and again I thought "what a gift!" To have this time, to feel this love, to know all would be well. It was quite a thing to be standing at the end of Tom's bed with his wife, his priest and a friend (all players in my own recovery) on the second anniversary of my cancer surgery. I had been celebrating at SeaWorld with my sister-in-law and niece when I got the call to come to Tom's bedside. Life is fragile. From one minute to the next, we don't know what's in store. And yet, moments like this reconfirm the gifts of faith and community and love for one another.

As we gathered for the funeral last night, I was talking with another Tom about all these gifts in the middle of the difficulties and he said to me "you know, it's all those God Box pray-ers at work that's made a difference." Funny, I hadn't thought of that! I just knew we were all "carried" somehow. Thanks for being the wind beneath our wings! Please continue to pray for Paula now as she adjusts to life without Tom, as she returns to work tomorrow, as she finds reliable transportation and gets her computer up and running. Thank you!

September 11, 2006
Good Morning on this 9/11 day of remembrance,
As I woke up this morning, I couldn't help but relive the rude awakening 5 years ago when my stepson David called to say he was ok. Ok . . . so it's good you're ok. Is something wrong? He was in NYC but *not* at a meeting in the World Trade Center because a business deal had fallen apart the night before. O happy failed business deal! He said things were chaotic and that planes were flying into buildings. We hadn't turned on TV yet so were oblivious about what was going on. Then it dawned on us that my niece Andrea could possibly be in NY because her flight attendant job takes here there several times a week. My brother and sister-in-law were in Europe. I felt my role move up a notch from Auntie to "on-call Mom" on a moment's notice. Then, as we were watching, the second plane hit. I called Andrea and got the message she recorded on her cell phone: she was in NYC, had flown in on American's last flight allowed to land and was safe. Oh my God. We were numb, confused, shaken, scared.

As we all tune in to "where we were on 9/11," let's pause for a moment to remember . . . and to recommit ourselves to healing the world. Thich Nhat Hanh offers a simple way: "Waking up this morning, I smile. Twenty-four brand new hours are before me. I vow to live fully in each moment and to look at all beings with eyes of compassion." I'm reminded, Peace IS the way . . .

November 6, 2006
Hello Everyone!
What an incredible week we have had here in the treetops. There are very few leaves left clinging to the branches. It is almost complete now. I named yesterday "recessional" as, one by one, the leaves waltzed their way to the earth. Today's title would have to be "still life" as no one is budging! Surrender has been the theme of the week. Surrender to the moment, to the process, to the unfolding that takes its own time. I am learning slowly to let go of productivity so that I can savor each moment. Finding a balance, struggling to feel less guilt, enjoying whatever presents itself . . . that has been the story of the week. And yes, I did write a few pages!

For openers, I'd like to share one of my "practice writes" with you. Perhaps it will provide *you* an opportunity to slow down and savor a moment. It's entitled "Good Morning!"

Cloudy skies and rain-washed trees greet me on this All Souls Day morning . . . and then a rush among the leaves that is the call of the deer! Good morning little one! Stopped in her tracks, she looks back at me and stares . . . seeming to be as interested in me as I in her. Locked gaze, one upon the other . . . Good morning! Yes, I am beautiful and graceful and awake. I delight you and you me. Yes, it is another day to explore and graze and awaken the senses to all the good around us. How is it that when I look for you, you are not there . . . and then when I am not looking, you surprise me. You come out of nowhere. So maybe it will be with words on paper, thoughts waiting beneath the surface to make their entry. When they come, I will delight and say, "Good morning little ones! Where have you been? Did you come to make my day? To delight my soul? To rise up and be noticed?

Like deer hiding in the woods, so are my thoughts, O Lord. Like deer gazing back, eye-to-eye, face-to-face, so my words will leap, page after page. Imagination is on the prowl—stopping here and there for a deep gaze, then taking flight across the page like deer across the field—lightly, gracefully, with direction, anticipation, delight.

Awaken my pen, skip, dance, twirl, begin!

December 25, 2006
Merry Christmas Everyone!
Darkness has given way to light and we are on the threshold of our Christmas celebration! Rejoice! I thank God for all the ways you have been a bright light for each other this year! I am reminded of a question from Meister Eckhart (13th Century Dominican mystic) . . . one that you answer with your generous lives: *"What good is it to me if Mary is full of grace and if I am not also full of grace? What good is it to me for the Creator to give birth to his Son if I do not also give birth to him in my time and in my culture?"*

At the beginning of Advent, I suggested spending a moment each day thinking of something we were grateful for both personally and in the world. Jerry and I have enjoyed this practice very much and hope to continue it in the new year! Today as I celebrate my 59th birthday, I am grateful to each of you for keeping me very much alive with your encouragement, your love and your prayers. It's an awesome thing to be held in loving kindness. Notice, I have no problem telling you my age. I rather enjoy seeing the number get bigger!

December 31, 2006
Happy New Year Everyone!
As we sit at the threshold of a new year, I am reminded of a Dec. 31 ritual in Los Angeles that I love. Jerry and I experienced it years ago, before we ever moved here. I don't know if it's still done (especially now that computers and Blackberries have replaced paper calendars for so many), but the image is still alive in my memory. As we walked through the downtown area, it seemed to be snowing! But the snow was not the cold, wet stuff we Wisconsinites know. It was calendar pages from those page-a-day desk calendars. As we looked up, it was like being in a huge 3-minute egg timer with the days of the previous year emptying out to pavement below . . . from one skyscraper office window, then another, and another. Some people hoisted the calendars out the windows with great vigor and a hurrah! . . . others just watched the pages float through the air like the leaves of fall letting go . . . saying their last good bye . . . giving way to something new. I felt like I was in a movie. It seemed surreal. It was its own meditation. *These* days of *this* year were gone. How had I spent them? What was I letting go of? What was dying . . . what was rising? What would fill the pages of the New Year's calendar?

The pages of our days write the stories of our lives. You have written a beautiful story with your gentle care and loving kindness for one another. You have stoked the coals of faith and hope for one another. *"I give thanks to my God at every remembrance of you, praying always with joy in my every prayer for all of you, because of your partnership for the gospel from that first day until now . . . and this is my prayer: that your love may increase ever more and more in knowledge and every kind of perception, to discern what is of value so that you may be pure and blameless for the day of Christ . . ."* (Phil. 1:3, 9)

February 5, 2007
Hi Everyone!
It is very early and I am writing to you from Irvine where we have front row seats for the delivery of our very first great niece! We drove up here after the Super Bowl last night and met my brother and sister-in-law and the proud parents-to-be. Andrea will be induced at 8 a.m. Such excitement! Such anticipation! I ask your prayers early today for a safe and easy delivery!

There is lots going on today that needs our wakeful attention. At 8:15 (PT) this morning our dear friend Mo will be having an MRI and at about 8 a.m. CST little Fiona (now 4 or 5, if my memory serves me) who had a brain tumor removed when she was a teeny tiny baby will also have a follow-up MRI.

In the past week, I experienced a bit of "dry bones" with my writing. Interestingly, I mentioned it to a couple people who immediately came to my rescue with chocolate and prayer and got me back on track with amazing speed. So . . . I don't hesitate to ask you all to keep praying for direction and a fluid pen (I did better with pen and paper vs. computer keys!). You don't have to send chocolate. Your prayers will suffice!

February 12, 2007
Hello Everyone!
What a wonderful week this has been! Last Monday, at 8 p.m. on the dot, my niece Andrea gave birth to a beautiful 8 pound 2.6 oz. baby girl. Welcome to our world sweet Milan Kassia (pronounced Ka-see' ah)! It was a long, laborious day but a little after 6 p.m. things began to happen. Andrea's Mom, her friend Beth and I were invited to witness the birth. What a miracle! I

can't begin to tell you what an emotionally awesome and joyful experience that was! Milan appeared on the scene with her little hand unfolding over her head saying hello to the world for the first time! WOW! This had to be one of the most incredible days of my life. What a privilege! Thanks to all of you for surrounding us with your love and prayers for a safe delivery and a healthy baby!

March 26, 2007
Good morning everyone! Happy Monday . . . another 24 hours to fill up with love and light . . . go for it! I'm writing to you today from Starbucks where I sit with a wonderful cup of fresh brewed coffee and a yummy scone . . . sweet rewards for more good test results, this time from my cardiologist. I just ran the treadmill to top speed and found that once again, all is well! With both parents and my brother going through multiple heart surgeries and having a tiny "electrical situation" myself, I see a cardiologist regularly . . . more preventatively than anything. Today it was the nurse who needed care more than I did. A single mom of a 13 year old, she discovered she has an aneurism on her brain. She has been in and out of the hospital for 2 weeks and is waiting now to see if she needs brain surgery. I was glad to hug her and to report that I have two friends who have successfully gone through brain surgery (what are the chances of that?!) . . . and that there is this thing I do called the God Box. "Yes," she sighed, "please put my name in the God Box." So, I ask your prayers for Theresa and her 13 year old son. May they have the courage and strength they need . . . and may they feel the love and support this virtual community so graciously offers.

April 17, 2007
Hello Everyone!
The God Box is a day late this week because I'm on the road and don't have easy access to the Internet. Lots has happened in a week and I find myself filled with both deep gratitude for so many personal blessings and with compassion for the horrible tragedy at Virginia Tech. I was in tears this afternoon as I watched TV coverage of the VT student assembly with their campus ministers offering words of comfort and hope and courage. I could see myself, my colleagues, and our own dear UCSD students in their faces. So much grief for young people to carry. So much healing needed. I was pleased to hear calls for a nonviolent

response, a strengthening of community ties, and the recognition that prayers from people who don't even know them will support and hold them. Let our prayers rise up like incense for the families and friends who lost loved ones and for all the students, faculty, and staff of Virginia Tech who will be dealing with this for a long time.

July 16, 2007

Good Monday morning, everyone! Hope you had a relaxing or festive weekend . . . or a chance to tend to the stuff of life! Being home for the whole weekend afforded me the opportunity to do a little gardening and cleaning. I don't know if it's because I've been doing a lot of reading about gratitude, but I found myself giving thanks as I trimmed bushes and cleaned the patio door tracks! As I pulled weeds along the garden's edge, I thought of all the edge-trimming I did for my Dad on Saturday mornings when he cut the grass . . . the kind of thing a kid can't mess up, but that teaches them how to take care of stuff. I smiled remembering my mother as I cleaned the patio door tracks. We didn't have patio doors when I was a kid, but we had lots of rain and that made for muddy window sills. That was another one of those little annoying, time-consuming jobs that parents handed off to kids! I found myself thanking my Mom and Dad for teaching me little things that made a difference . . . things that taught me organization, consistency, self-reliance, and care for the things of the earth. Later on Saturday, I chatted away the night with our Julie about all these little remembrances . . . and was grateful for the opportunity to smile once more as I remembered my folks.

August 6, 2007

Good Morning Everyone! Our visitors are still sleeping (ah sweet vacation pleasures!), so I have a few minutes to tend to the God Box. We have been having such a great time enjoying all things summer that I didn't realize until this morning that today is the 62nd anniversary of the bombing of Hiroshima and Nagasaki. I invite you to pause for a moment of silence after reading this little piece from gratefulness.org:

August 6: A somber, prayerful remembrance of the victims of the atomic bombs dropped on Hiroshima and Nagasaki (August 6 and 9, 1945). Many people follow the Japanese custom of sailing paper lanterns with peace prayers inscribed on them down streams and rivers.

More than 270,000 people died as a result of the atomic bombs dropped on Hiroshima and Nagasaki in August 1945. These bombs are now considered, along with all weapons of mass destruction, as a crime against humanity. In addition to our prayers for peace today, we recommit ourselves to working for peace with all our heart and strength. As Brother David Steindl-Rast writes in Gratefulness, the Heart of Prayer: "Since August 6, 1945, no one can deny that all of us belong together in this spaceship Earth. 'When you are in the same boat with your worst enemy, will you drill a hole into his side of the boat?' asks Elissa Melamed."

This remembrance and a letter we received from Sean who is serving in Iraq caused me to stop in my vacation tracks to realize that while we are enjoying fun in the sun, so many of our young people are in harm's way under that same hot sun. I am reminded how much our prayers for peace need to continue. And I invite us all to recommit to praying for peace every day at 9:00 p.m. (EST).

October 22, 2007

Good Tuesday Morning from a remote location! The fires continue to rage in San Diego, and we are safe at the Best Western Mission Bay hotel. Miss Tilly, our cat, is with us . . . and hides under the bed most of the time. She's more open with her feelings! 350,000 people have been evacuated (mandatory) thus far. They expect a half million by end of day. Last night we decided to voluntarily evacuate so we could rest a little easier as the fickle winds continued to gust. We slept much better. Thanks so much for all the love and prayers you are sending our way. I checked my email before we left last night and felt a real boost from all the messages we received. This note from Michael helped me realize why we felt so protected. "I am bringing myself and the people that I meet to a place of calm and peace. That calm and peace, my form of prayer, will balance out the winds of the region. Be as peaceful as you can in this fury, and the calm will come to the region. Get as many as possible to be peaceful too, and the balance will occur." It was amazingly clear all day long in El Cajon. I felt like we were living in a bubble! I invite you to join Mike et al. in expanding the circle of peace and calm.

Our dear friends Ginny and David are on a cruise in Hawaii as their little village of Crest is under mandatory evacuation. You might remember that theirs was one of a couple homes left standing in the 2004 fires as their daughter's home below them was lost. Pam just moved back in about a year ago. I can't imagine what it would feel like to be evacuated after all that.

Little Savannah, my cousin's preemie, who we prayed from 1.5 pounds to baptism at about six pounds last year, was on the move yesterday morning as she and her parents were evacuated. They are faring well in a hotel in La Jolla.

As you can imagine, there is a whole range of emotion that comes with this kind of situation. Sunday night I found myself feeling anxious throughout the night . . . calling out to God just as I did when I found out I had cancer . . . singing the "Keep Me Safe O God" in my head and keeping one eye open so we'd be ready to evacuate at any minute. The reverse 911 call system has been working very well to wake people up and get them out in time. I found it hard to focus on little else all day . . . just waiting and watching . . . trying to stay peaceful . . . but not wanting to be naïve to the danger. Soaking up all the suffering, I was reminded of a Lenten reflection from Ron Rolheiser who talked about Jesus taking in all the chaos, holding it, and bringing compassion and order to it. It's what I try to do . . . but it is a process!!

October 25, 2007
Hi Everyone!
Jer and I came home yesterday to a house still standing! We are filled with gratitude for a thousand things like winds that lose their breath, firefighters who never give up, preplanning that makes things work, leaders who find the resources, volunteers who show up, a stadium that can shelter thousands of people at once, officials who let it happen, clowns and musicians who lighten the atmosphere, DC-10s that spread acres of fire retardant at a time, clergy and doctors who mend hearts and heal wounds, love, kindness, and grace all around. San Diego is alive and well!

October 29, 2007
Hi Everyone!
We are slowly getting back to the more normal rhythms of life in San Diego after the fires. It has been great to be with the people we love and to tell the stories, to feel the release of fears, to hold one another again—perhaps more tenderly—and to breathe in all the goodness around us. On Saturday night, we had our neighbors over for dessert and coffee to celebrate our gratitude that our neighborhood is still standing and so are we! We thank you for all the love and prayers you sent our way and ask that you continue praying for all those who lost their homes or their loved ones. According to today's newspaper, an estimated 640,000 people were forced to evacuate; more than 1500 of those homes were reduced to ashes. 7 people died in the fires and there were a few more fire-related deaths. Many civilians and firefighters have been hurt; some are in critical condition with severe burns.

We are expecting some mild to moderate Santa Ana winds on Friday and Saturday so we ask you to pray, meditate, focus your energy on this area some more. Fires are still burning in some areas, though many are contained—some more than others. My friend Michael offers this hopeful research: *I have uncovered some research that validates that when 1% of a population sits in meditation the collective consciousness is balanced and that violence in all forms (fires included) decreases 25% and that cooperation and creativity increases 68%. The people don't even have to be together during the meditation.* Are you willing to be part of that 1%?

January 21, 2008
Hi everyone! Hope your Monday morning is off to a good start on this Martin Luther King holiday, and that you are reflecting on ways to keep the MLK dream alive. We had a wonderful celebration at the Catholic Community at UCSD yesterday. Our choir picketed the church with signs like those carried in civil rights demonstrations in the '60s, and then they marched in for Mass singing *We Shall Overcome.* Maureen from our Resident Community introduced a clip from MLK's speech, *"Beyond Vietnam: A Time to Break Silence"* (which has lessons for Iraq), by sharing her own experience of marching on Washington in 1963 when MLK gave his *I Have a Dream* speech. You could hear a pin drop in the church!

March 3 2008
Hi Everyone!
We had a wonderful time at the LA Religious Ed Congress this weekend! It was such an explosion of energy and creativity and insight and hope! I finally got to hear Paula D'Arcy speak. I had read about her while on sabbatical last year . . . and had found hope in the fact that she had at least 8 rejections from publishers before *Crossroads* picked up her best-selling book *Gift of the Red Bird*! Her session, entitled "What's Enough?" provided further inspiration for my Lenten attempt to de-clutter my life! I knew I liked her right away when she quoted from one of my favorite authors, Ted Loder (often cited in the God Box).

When Paula was 27 years old and pregnant, she, her husband and her 21 month old daughter were struck by a drunk driver. Only she and her unborn daughter survived. *Gift of the Red Bird* chronicles her grief. On Saturday she said, "Life offers its wisdom generously. Stay awake! Play the hand that's been dealt to you (it's enough!) . . . Unless you tame your demons, you'll never know your angels!" Her 33 year old daughter was there in the 3rd row. I can only imagine how much admiration pulsed through her as she heard her mother speak.

Another speaker, Fr. Donald Cozzens, nudged us to claim some solitude each day, noting that all the evil in the world can be traced to our inability to sit still. One of the most important things we can do to survive, he said, is to sit still. Then we'll become instruments of healing; our presence will become a healing presence.

March 17, 2008
Happy St. Patty's Day . . . Blessed beginning of Holy Week . . . and exam week at UCSD . . . and somber greetings as we recognize the fifth anniversary of the War in Iraq. So many things tug at our attention. In the midst of that Jer has invited me (vs. bugging me!!) to go out to Borrego Dessert today because we are at the peak of the *flower season* out there! So . . . I have to practice what I preach . . . "Don't just *do* something, *sit* there!"

On Saturday we participated in a march and rally for peace in City Heights sponsored by the San Diego Coalition for Justice and Peace. As we approached the intersection where the crowd was gathering, I realized I'd forgotten to make a sign (duh . . .). Just then, the young man who was hurrying toward the crowd as we parked, plunked down the many signs he was carrying and invited us to take one. My eyes were immediately attracted to a huge computer picture of Jesus pasted on a 3 foot piece of cardboard with the words: "Who would Jesus bomb?" Good question. Never mind I didn't like the artwork . . . I picked up the sign and joined the cheering throng. Jer's sign said "The war is over . . . if you want it to be." Hmmm . . . we make choices, don't we? Others were simple: "Enough!" and "Peace Now" or "Paz Pronto." Some were not so kind . . . and even though I understand the anger, I squirm a bit at character assaults and degradation, *especially* at a peace rally. Gandhi's "We must become the change we want to see in the world" haunts me. I was overcome with emotion as we lined University Ave at Fairmont . . . . choking back tears as we shouted: What do you want? Peace! When do you want it? Now! and as we sang "All we are saying, is give peace a chance!" A 10-foot tall papier mache headed figure of an Iraqi woman with flowing veil wove her way through the crowd, carrying a bloodied rag doll baby. The numbers are as staggering as she was . . . 1,200,000 Iraqi deaths caused by US invasion, 4,000 American Soldier deaths, $493,000,000,000 (that's half a trillion!) spent so far.

The Agony in the Garden continues . . . and I take all this into the desert of Holy Week with me.

April 14, 2008
Hello Everyone!
We had a wonderful and meaningful weekend as we participated in the *Relay for Life* at UCSD under sunny skies and 80 degree temps! I cried my way all the way around the track during The Survivors' Lap as I again recognized how grateful I am to be alive and to be supported by so many wonderful people (some who were there)!! Our Student Ministry team and others from the Catholic Community at UCSD lined the track as I walked side-by-side with Mark (one of our Student Ministers), the mother of another student and a woman from my support group. We helped carry the banner for the American Cancer Society. *Relay for Life*, we were told, is the largest fundraising event of its kind in the entire world! It is expected that this event at UCSD will raise $70,000 . . . and lots of awareness. Thirty other relays are planned for San Diego alone this year!

In the evening, Jer and I went back to participate in the Luminaria Ceremony to remember all those who have died. This was the time to remember and to grieve. I was invited to give the talk for this "Remembering" part of the event. In it, I especially remembered my best girlfriend, Marilyn, who died of breast cancer at age 49, and I honored Annie, our other best girlfriend who is surviving after her encounter with thyroid cancer just last month. Three out of three best friends all affected by cancer! More tears! Luminarias lined the track in memory of those who have died and in honor of those who are surviving. Quite a meditation to see all the names painted on the luminarias of mothers and fathers, grandparents, aunts and uncles, brothers and sisters and dear friends. In the bleachers, luminarias spelled out the word HOPE. And that's what we felt as we walked another mile by candlelight and remembered all those for whom we have been praying.

May 12, 2008
Happy Benign Monday Morning!
Yes, the news is good! Once again, I do not have breast cancer! While I felt confident that was the case, there's always a little "hedge" until the results come in. I always feel that *no matter what*, "all will be well," but I also realize that it could take some work . . . and readiness! I am humbled by all those who are in treatment, and I am in constant awe of several women in my support group who have faced multiple cancers: breast cancer, then ovarian cancer, then breast cancer again . . . or in another case, ovarian, then ovarian, then ovarian again. Breast cancer and ovarian cancer are linked by the same gene. That's why they did the biopsy for me . . . even though there was a 98% chance it was nothing. Once again, I am reminded to make today count. *This* is the day that the Lord has made . . . . *Rejoice and be glad in it!!*

June 12, 2008
My Dear Friends and Family . . .
I woke up on Wednesday morning with gut-wrenching pain that was so deep and pervasive and raw that I didn't know where else to turn but to the same God who filled me with so much joy on Monday . . . and to *you*, my dear friends and family. My only brother whom I love so much died suddenly on Tuesday at about 5 p.m. Jerry called me home from work because he had something he needed to talk with me about *right away.* He refused to give me any clues.

I couldn't imagine what was going on . . . but I went home immediately. All the way home I went through a whole laundry list of things that could have happened. I went numb when Jerry told me it was Steve.

We are sad . . . we are crying lots . . . we are holding each other up. I know that my brother is held in the hands of God . . . and my dear parents . . . and is perfectly, utterly safe. I ask you please to shower our family with your love and prayers . . . especially my dear sister-in-law, Diana, my niece Andrea, and sweet Milan who will never know her incredible Grandpa.

July 4, 2008
We're back!
We had a wonderful trip to Beijing and Bangkok. I thank God and Steve *and all of you* for helping us to find a way through our grief to let go enough to enjoy each blessed present moment. The pain of our loss was numbed a little . . . and processed a little as we found ourselves lighting incense and spinning prayer wheels at Buddhist temples . . . all the while humming good little Catholic tunes like "Let my prayer rise up like incense before you . . ." While Catholics are known for "smells and bells," I think the Buddhists have out-incensed us by far! It was intriguing to get inside the Buddhist spirituality and to witness the fervor, devotion and practice of the Chinese and Thai people. Our prayers for you and for all the intentions in the God Box were spun out again and again, as was our gratitude. Besides visiting numerous temples and seeing the Gold Buddha, the reclining Buddha, the tall Buddha, the laughing Buddha, etc., we walked the Great Wall, toured the Forbidden City, walked through so many majestic parks and palaces, climbed thousands of steep steps to the Drum and Bell Towers, rickshawed through the houtongs (old neighborhoods of Beijing), rode long boats through the floating markets of Bangkok, sipped tea, drank Chinese beer and tried all kinds of intriguing foods . . . minus the frogs!

Our chopsticks have been retired and we are back to the future now . . . which is all about returning to work to clean out my office, and clearing the deck to resume writing my book! Our stamina and energy have been great . . . and for this, too, we are grateful!

August 4, 2008
Hello Dear Friends,
It was tough to leave the beach. Nothing like waking up to the sound of the pounding waves and the morning call of the seagull. We are back home now, renewed and refreshed and mindful once again of all the *homey* things that refresh us as well. With all the talk of "staycations" (staying at home and saving on gas), I can't help but think of my dear mother with gratitude for all the ways she helped us appreciate good company and home with all those games of Scrabble and Canasta she played with my girlfriends and me at our kitchen table. She knew instinctively what Thich Nhat Hanh tells us: "Invest in yourself and your child . . . Be a friend to his friends; participate as much as you can in his life." My mom and dad did that in a thousand ways. Perhaps it was in honor of them that we spent Saturday night on the patio with friends, eating by candlelight, then going inside for another round of Scrabble! Waves and seagulls are wonderful, so is summer porch sitting and playing games at home!

August 11, 2008
Hi Everyone! Amazing, isn't it, that sometimes the week we have planned takes an entirely different course. Sickness and death do that . . . change our course. Last Monday I had plans to have my dear friends, Marge (89 with cancer) and Jean (her best buddy), over for a little patio sitting and dinner. Marge didn't feel well enough to come, and by Wed. we were setting up hospice home care for her and I somehow became the person in charge. Not what she had planned . . . not what I had planned . . . but what is is, and there we were doing life another way. We are now pretty well set up with about 25 volunteers who are keeping her company and tending to her needs 24/7.

RE Jenny: I can't help but think of Jenny often these days as I watch broadcasts of the Beijing Olympics. Most of you will remember that this dear friend (former youth rep for the Archdiocese of Milwaukee when I worked there) was in a life-changing accident Aug. 22, 2007, as she was training to win a likely spot on the U.S. Olympic long distance running team. Jenny continues to make progress, and continues to need our prayers as she trains vigorously for the rest of her life. With every Olympic event you watch, please be mindful of Jenny, and ask God's healing for her.

August 18, 2008
Happy Monday Evening!
As I begin this very late edition of the God Box, I am reminded of an old childhood commercial: *It's 11:00 p.m . . . . Parents do you know where your children are?"* Hmmm . . . . sort of like *"Friends, it's 7 p.m . . . . do you know where your God Box is?"*

Jer and I camped out with our friend Marge last night who is living out her final days. She was asleep when we arrived at 9 p.m. and only woke up once . . . not to cough . . . but to talk . . . long into the night about obstacles to true peace. I pray, and ask you to pray with me, for Marge's peaceful death. In the morning, I stole away to an appointment while Jerry kept vigil until the morning crew arrived. It is such a beautiful thing to see so many people involved in keeping Marge company 24/7. All those structures we work so hard to build and sustain . . . like small church communities, the parish outreach group, women's group, the Morning Mass group, etc. have all come together to ease this beautiful person into paradise. The love, the care, the sacrifice . . . all are so tangible and beautiful to behold. And, we can feel all the love and prayers you are providing . . . as the wind beneath our wings.

September 22, 2008
Fall is in the air . . . and at our feet (though we Californians don't have as many leaves to shuffle and crunch through as those "back east!") The hours of light and dark are exactly equal on this first day of fall. We are letting go of summer's longer days of fun in the sun and moving toward darker days. We are entering the season of transformation . . . from death to life . . . but death must come first. And so it was for my dear friend Margie. She completed her earthly cycle and entered eternal life on Saturday at 10:25 a.m. And now she rests in peace. Thanks be to God . . . and to you for your prayers! I was scheduled to be with her from 11 a.m. – 1 p.m. and so arrived just after she passed. Carol, the wonderful woman who brought the Eucharist to her each day was there when she died, as were two hospice nurses who were "changing guard." I am so happy Carol was there . . . representing our community, and standing as a symbol for the nourishment she received in bread broken and love shared. I stayed with her son and a couple others as her diminished body was prepared to leave its earthy dwelling place. It was sobering to witness Marge's final bow . . . leaving

her home in her friend's freshly washed pj's, wrapped snuggly in a clean white sheet, carried out by "stranger" arms with a promise that she'd be cared for lovingly. Familiar melodies and phrases played in my head: "Into your hands, I commend my Spirit O Lord" . . . and "It is finished."

It is an interesting phenomenon how one moves from such profound mysteries back into the mundanity of life. It took a few hours before I could do much besides stumble around. Telling the story of her passing to those who had kept vigil helped some. As one friend said, "Margie was the poster child for dying well." She couldn't bypass the suffering, but she was surrounded with love, and I believe we helped her bridge the gap between heaven and earth. With Margie "safely home" in heaven, we moved on to house cleaning and ceiling fan installations! Ah the sweet beat of life!

Appendix B:

Savannah in the God Box

Some people are better known than others in *The God Box*. Little Savannah, my cousin's baby, is one of them. Her surprise entry into the world four months earlier than expected got everyone's attention. She weighed in at just one and a half pounds. Her arms were so tiny that her dad's wedding ring could be slipped up over her shoulder. For months, the God Box Community watched and waited and prayed for Savannah. If I wasn't reporting on her progress, I was being asked about it! This virtual community of loving kindness had never met Savannah, yet they surrounded her and her parents with unbounded prayer and affection. As Brian and Erica held Savannah in the palm of their hands, they were being carried on eagle's wings. They were holding her, holding on, and being held all at once.

Ten months after Savannah was born, she was baptized. My husband Jerry and I were chosen to be her godparents. Somehow, I felt like I was just standing in for a whole community of godmothers and godfathers who helped breathe life into this little girl. Many of them were standing there with us to welcome Savannah into our faith community. Virtual Community *live*!

Here is Savannah's story as it appeared in the pages of *The God Box* and as it was presented to her on the day of her baptism. With it came a big candle to light on her birthdays in remembrance of all the candles that were lit for her and her very own God Box[33] to stash prayers of her own one day.

Savannah's God Box

Presented to her by her Godparents, Lynn and Jerry Neu,
on the occasion of her Baptism, November 26, 2006

Dear Sweet Savannah,

Welcome to the Catholic Community! It is with great joy that we celebrate your baptism today in a community that is seeing you for the first time but that has been praying for you from the day you were born. You have taught them so much already about the fragility of life, dependence on God, the power of prayer, the benefits of living in community, and the joy of watching God's wonder at work.

Today water is poured over your little head—cleansing, refreshing, renewing, nourishing water—a sign of your life in Christ. And sweet-smelling oil is signed as a cross on your little forehead—strengthening, empowering, regal oil of kings and queens—a sign of your importance, God's favor, and your strength in God. And you receive a lighted candle—burning brightly, giving light in darkness, calling you to be light to the world just like Jesus.

We, your godparents, promise to support you in your faith journey and to be there for you in times of joy and in times of struggle. We offer you this little book at the beginning of that journey to give you an idea of how you were held by so many faith-filled people in the very first days of your life. It is a collection of excerpts from "The God Box," a weekly email that Lynn sent out asking people to pray for you. We hope that you will be inspired by God's love and the love of the "God Box" community. You are cherished and loved by so many!

Savannah "in the God Box"

Savannah makes her entrance into the world much sooner than expected.

January 20, 2006

Hi Everyone,

Another very full God Box . . . with many people waiting for the comfort of your powerful prayers . . .
Let us pray for:

- Cousin Erica who delivered a premature baby girl Wednesday night, weighing just 1 1/2 pounds. Pray for this little bundle's strength and for faith and courage for Erica and Brian.

January 30, 2006
- Brian and Erica's baby Savannah Renee (at 1 1/2 pounds) continues to do well . . . even after heart surgery to close off that little heart valve. I'll forward her mom's latest email that has a picture so you can see who you are praying for.

February 6, 2006
- Savannah's blood gas levels slipped a bit this weekend. She had to be reintubated. Earlier in the week she'd been taken off the respirator and seemed so strong. She's a fighter . . . but needs lots of prayers beneath her tiny wings. Please pray for Brian and Erica's emotional and spiritual strength, too.

Special prayers are always part of "The God Box." This one was included on Feb. 6

I Praise You for What is Yet to Be

Wondrous Worker of Wonders,
I praise you

not alone for what has been,
   or for what is,
   but for what is yet to be,
for you are gracious beyond all telling of it . . .

I praise you
that you turn me loose
   to go with you to the edge of now and maybe,
     to welcome the new,
       to see my possibilities,
         to accept my limits,
and yet begin living to the limit
  of passion and compassion
    until,
      released by joy,
I uncurl to other people
  and to your kingdom coming,
for you are gracious beyond all telling of it.
          —Ted Loder, *Guerrillas of Grace*, 1984, Innisfree Press

Sometimes, I sent special updates from your mom to all those who were praying for you . . . here are a couple of them . . .

January 25, 2006, Savannah's Heart Surgery

Savannah had heart surgery at 5 days old on Monday afternoon. This was to close up the extra heart valve that would normally close up if she had waited. She did fine, and didn't lose even a thimble of blood. She is as stable as can be expected and is still doing everything she should be doing considering. Both yesterday and the day before, we were able to get there for her "touch time"—the only time they touch her to limit overstimulation. She opened her eyes for us. I got to change her diaper—the only time I will be excited about a diaper change. =)
Thank you for all of your prayers and support.

~Erica & Brian

February 6, 2006 Update on Savannah
Hello everyone!
Ok, the past few days have produced a lot of excitement! On Tuesday night, the doctor decided to take advantage of Savannah's strong stats and they took her off of the respirator! =) She is now on what is called a C-Pap which monitors her breathing and gives her small puffs of air to ensure expansion of her lungs. She doesn't like the prongs up her nose, but then again, who would?

Then yesterday morning, Savannah decided to demand more attention than necessary and set off a bunch of bells and whistles. This alarmed everyone enough to think she needed to go back on the respirator for a little longer (which is common). After 10 minutes of trying, Savannah was not having it and actually would not let them stick that tube back down her throat. So continuing with the C-Pap it was! They made some modifications to the C-Pap to assist with her breathing a slight bit more, and so far, all is good! They did opt to give her some additional medication to help her lungs grow and develop, but other than that, she is continuing to prove that she is feisty and definitely a fighter! =)

Thank you for all of your support and prayers. Here are the current forecasted goals:

- Savannah needs to gain at least 20 grams a day. If this happens, then ideally she will be able to come home before her actual due date (May 8th).
- The C-Pap gets taken off, and Savannah graduates to what is called a nasal canula—small oxygen tube with the nose prongs.
- With the removal of the C-Pap, the Arterial I.V. line gets removed and only one of her hands is boarded up with an I.V. in it. (Hopefully this happens within the next couple of days.)

~Erica and Brian

February 14, 2006
Hello all!
Well, I know it's been a while since the last update, but here it goes. Savannah is doing really well with her feedings and her digestive track is processing

everything really well on its own. Her respiratory problems have been on the swing. She has been fighting a pneumonia called microplasma which is causing her lungs to be really wet and have a major challenge expanding enough to intake enough oxygen for her blood. They have had to place her back on the hi-frequency respirator, and have been giving her some breathing treatments kind of like you would for someone who has asthma.

The cool thing is that thanks to our friend, Megan, Savannah is little Miss Fashion Diva of the NICU, and the talk of the Nurses! Check out her outfit! =) This is something Megan found online that is handmade by a lady in all places—Tacoma, WA. It is made to fit Micro-preemies between 1 & 2.5 lbs.

The other really neat thing was that Brian and I both had an opportunity to hold her last week before she ended up back on the Hi-frequency. It was AWESOME!!! They call it Kangaroo Care because you hold her skin-to-skin like a kangaroo would with their young.

Well, until the next update, keep up the thoughts and prayers!
~Erica, Brian & Savannah!

More Updates in the God Box . . .

February 21, 2006
Tiny Savannah is holding her own, though she has her little ups and downs.

March 6, 2006
Yoohoo for little Savannah! Last week she graduated to a nasal cannula (typical oxygen tube you see on most hospitalized patients) and weighed in at 1000 grams (still under 2 pounds). She maintained her weight for 2 days and has attained "feeder/grower" status! She'll be transferred back to Scripps Hospital where she was born (she's been at Children's Hospital's special unit). Now she needs to learn to suck, swallow, and breathe all at once so she can grow to 1,500–1,600 grams. Then her mom and dad can hold her for more than an hour once a day. Erica says, "Thanks for the prayers! Clearly, they are helping!"

March 19, 2006

Today I went to baby Savannah's shower and saw new pictures of her as well as her little foot and handprints! She's beginning to look like both her mom and her dad and is growing about an ounce a day. They are hoping she'll be able to go home at the end of April. Lots of little daily goals to accomplish between now and then, so keep praying! After today's shower, we decided that she's already spoiled!

May 1, 2006

From Erica: When will little **Savannah** go home? "Hopefully within a week. I am definitely anxious. I think I will be like a kid at Christmas once they finally give us a definite date. Until then, poor Savannah needs to build up her energy so she can take all other feedings by bottle."

May 8, 2006

Hi Everyone!

In the spirit of yesterday's great news that Savannah can go home, I thought it appropriate to begin this edition of The God Box with this "Psalm to Virgin Spring:"

> *Drawn upward by some hidden power,*
> *life is crackling the crust of earth*
> *and bursting forth from limb and stem.*
> *Your aroma, O Life-giver,*
> *is upon the springtime wind,*
> *and I feel its power*
> *stirring deep within me.*
>
> *Green is your color, O God,*
> *the green of new life*
> *that lovingly transfigures earth's dreariness,*
> *long held prisoner*
> *by the icy web of winter's cold.*
>
> *Green up my heart with hope,*
> *in your perpetual promise of life.*

Send forth from my soul
new shoots, fresh buds
eager to grow in your divine image.

—Edward Hays, *Prayers for a Planetary Pilgrim*

In the spirit of spring's new life, this week we have this to celebrate: Savannah is eating better!

May 15, 2006
RE SAVANNAH: I got to hold her lots on Friday and felt so good about her energy, strength, beauty, and adaptability. I couldn't help but think of all of you and your tremendous outpouring of interest, love, and support as I held her. *Thank you!* She's eating well and growing day by day. Keep praying that her mom and dad get the rest they need to keep up with her. More photos soon!

June 6, 2006
I had the privilege of being with little Savannah and her mom, Erica, yesterday. You'll be happy to know that Savannah is weighing in at 6 pounds 9 ounces and is adjusting well to life at home with Mom and Dad! Grandma Ginny was there last week to lend a hand—no both hands—and give Erica a little rest. Erica is such a good mom—tender, loving, patient—giving her all to give this little one the best. Brian is usually at work when I'm there, but I know him well enough to know he's a good daddy!

I have to tell you about getting Savannah settled down last night after her feeding. She suffers from a bit of acid reflux after eating so gets a little fussy. Once we got Erica down for a nap, I began my walk with Savannah. I swear, soon as I began humming "Hail Mary, Gentle Woman" to her, she stopped crying, breathed more evenly and just relaxed in my arms. It was like I'd flipped a switch! Granted, the switch went off and on a few times but, it was pretty amazing that first time! I couldn't help but feel surrounded by all of you who have surrounded her with your love and prayers as well as Mother Mary and all those who have gone before us—her grandpa (my mother's brother), my mom and dad, Marilyn, oh-so-many saints and angels watching over us loving this little girl to sleep. It was one of those magic moments, and you were all there with us!

July 24, 2006
Please pray for my cousin **Erica** who goes back to work next week and is still looking for the best caretaker for **Savannah**. She has something lined up, but it's not ideal.

Closing prayer for July 24:

Psalm 20

> May the One who created you in
> wholeness
> meet your needs when you call!
> May the Name of Love be your
> protection
> and rise up in your heart as a
> tower of strength!
> May all you have given in gratitude
> and with open hands
> be returned to you a hundredfold!
> May your heart's desires and all
> your plans
> be fulfilled in due season!

Here is the last entry before your Baptism, but not the last time we'll be remembering you, I'm sure!

November 20, 2006

For our dear little Savannah who will "completely" celebrate her baptism with the Catholic Community on Sunday *(after her "emergency" baptism without the community on January 18 as she weighed in at 1 ½ pounds)*. Jerry and I are honored to be her godparents! She's weighing in at over 11 pounds now.

Appendix C:

Bonus Box

Some things just need to be shared! Here are a few of my favorite things that have either appeared in the God Box or crossed my path at just the right time.

ATTITUDE IS EVERYTHING!

Lucky Seven House Rules

This is a house of LIFE. Here we practice the fine art of living.

1. We live each day as if our lives have just begun. Every day comes with GOALS, and we do our best to meet or exceed them. Each sunrise marks a fresh start.

2. ATTITUDE is everything. If yours happens to be negative or pessimistic today, see an attitude-readjustment specialist before giving us a call.

3. We crack JOKES in this house, so be prepared to tease and be teased. If you have thin skin, wear a parka.

4. Cancer sucks, so crying is okay. Sobs are even better (they get the gunk out). And sobs followed by unstoppable LAUGHTER are the best!

5. This is a house of HEALING—mind, body and spirit. Positive, strong, hopeful energy circulates here.

6. PRAYERS are most welcome in this house. God has blessed us in so many ways, and together we have made—and continue to make—miracles happen every day.

Story behind "The Lucky Seven House Rules":

From Ken, July 24, '06: We had a rather unexpected setback this week with the results of Dad's brain MRI . . . some tumors on his cerebellum held or reduced in size . . . but others were resistant and have grown . . . Considering chemo options, side effects and compromised immune system . . . . Meanwhile, more tumors in his spine . . . Hoping to reduce pain and retain quality of life . . . Our request this week is that you turn your positive thoughts and prayers on HIGH so that Dad can discern his future with as much clarity, grace and peace as possible . . . In the event that we're at the end of the line in terms of the help that medical science can offer, we've started exploring alternative holistic therapies, including massage, meditation, etc. We surround ourselves with positive people and positive energy, and we continue to follow the "House Rules," living one day at a time and each day to the fullest. And we pray—a LOT. We know we're doing everything we humanly can to save Dad's life—the rest is in God's hands.

Being Open to Experience (Internet "forward," source unknown)

That some good can be derived from every event is a better proposition than that everything happens for the best, which it assuredly does not.

—James K. Feibleman

As the credit-card ad says, "Life comes at you fast." We don't get to pick all of our experiences. Life will give us some that are nice, and some that are not so nice, some that are easy and some that are hard. The difference is partly in the nature of the events and partly in how we respond to them. We naturally want to avoid accidents, natural disasters, illness, and death, but the way we handle them when they occur makes all the difference. It is possible to spoil every experience, good or bad, by taking a victim perspective. It is possible to transform every painful experience through acceptance and equanimity.

Every unfortunate event carries with it an opportunity. It may be the opportunity to learn better coping skills, or it may be the opportunity to test our patience and courage. Perhaps it is the opportunity to refocus our attention on what matters or to draw closer to the people that matter most to us.

We can easily miss those opportunities by dwelling on our special misery. When we make it all about ourselves, when ego takes center stage, when we focus on the question, "Why me?" and on the unfairness of it all, we only deepen our suffering. Some questions are unanswerable, and some of them are not useful. When catastrophe happens, it is natural to ask, "Why did this happen to me?" Sometimes the answer is apparent: "I smoked for thirty years." "I rode my bike without a helmet." "I treated people like dirt." "I was in a hurry packing my chute." In other circumstances, the cause of the disaster is not apparent. It seems random, unfair, and inexplicable. In such a case the better question is, "Given that this has happened, how shall I proceed?"

When faced with the "Why me?" question. The answer may be "Why not me?" Am I so special that I don't have to face the problems other people have also? Whatever we are experiencing, it is highly probable that someone else has had worse. People with fewer resources than we have likely faced equal or greater difficulty. We are each one among billions of humans faced with the dilemma of suffering. The more useful questions may be:

How can I face this challenge with equanimity and grace?

How can I access my courage—not lack of fear, but accepting and transcending fear?

How can I be more focused on gratitude?

What is still good despite the bad?

What supports me in this hardship?

What remains beautiful amidst this ugliness?

What is to be learned by this? How can I use that?

healthjourneys

Resources for Mind, Body and Spirit.

Belleruth Naparstek

I am a real fan of Belleruth Naparstek. I used her CD, "For People Undergoing Chemotherapy," as I began treatment. I can't begin to tell you what a difference it made. I relaxed and engaged my powerful mind to assist me in the healing process. By my second round of chemo, I felt as if the cancer was gone and that I was just going through the motions. I encourage anyone facing cancer, surgery, chemotherapy, or other health challenges to visit her Web site, **www.healthjourneys.com**, where you'll find this description of services offered:

Health Journeys is a private, multimedia publishing company, owned and operated since its inception in 1991 by George R. Klein and Belleruth Naparstek. The company produces and distributes Health Journeys and other guided imagery and meditation tapes, CDs, books, and software—in other words, holistic health tools that teach healing and wellness practices.

Large quantities of Health Journeys titles are custom-branded for distribution by hospitals, HMOs, insurance carriers, patient-advocacy organizations, government agencies, employee wellness programs, and pharmaceutical companies. In addition, a dedicated network of over 1,200 holistic health practitioners resells our titles to their patients and clients.

BR's 13 (Lucky) Tips for De-stressing Your Holidays

Belleruth Naparstek, Health Journeys, Nov. 23, 2007, www.healthjourneys.com

1. **Take Care of Your Body**
    Try to do all those things you know are good for your physical well being: get regular exercise; take it easy on the caffeine, sugar and alcohol; get enough sleep; eat healthy food—you know this stuff. This is the baseline of stress reduction.

2. **Track Your Physical Comfort**
    Take time to check in and see how your body is feeling. Once you notice, you can make small corrections to relieve discomfort before it takes over. Breathe into tight places; stretch and move when your back or neck feels stiff; look out the window when your eyes are straining at the computer screen; massage your neck and press the acupoints when a headache is lurking. But you have to notice what's amiss first.

3. **Learn to Relax at Will**
    Develop a regular practice to ground and relax you. If possible, start and end the day with guided imagery, yoga, meditation, relaxation, deep breathing, petting the cat in a rocking chair or listening to soothing music. Even five minutes, twice a day, will give you some protective ballast against the day's stresses. And if you can't manage this daily, do it whenever you can.

4. **Take a Mini-break When You're Getting Crazed**
    When you find yourself starting to lose it, or butting up against your own rigidity or circular thinking, take a quick break. Step away. Go outside for a walk, do some guided imagery, snuggle your favorite toddler, play some music, call a loving friend or do a couple of yoga stretches. Five minutes of conscious AWOL can clear your mind and give you back your perspective, flexibility and common sense.

5. **Dose Your Day with Humor**
    Humor, by its nature, provides instant distance, balance and perspective, if even for a moment. As long as it's not aimed at mocking

others, it allows us to step back and take everything, including ourselves, less seriously. So practice the art of finding the ludicrous, paradoxical and nonsensical in daily events. And laughing itself is priceless. A belly laugh changes biochemistry and clears out emotional gunk like little else.

6. **Be Realistic & Know Your Limits**
    It's a wonderful thing to know what you can and cannot do. Wrestle your perfectionism to the ground and don't let idealized expectations press you into doing more than you can realistically manage. Say no. Set limits. Work smart. This is especially important around holiday time, when trying too hard to do too much creates the exact opposite of the holiday feeling you're striving for, and you morph into the cranky, resentful, martyred, overworked nightmare you swore you'd never be.

7. **Manage Your Time**
    A corollary is to try not to over-commit. If you do, make a list and prioritize. (Just getting these things out of your head and onto a piece of paper will reduce some stress.) If the list is out of control, look it over and assess what has to go—and then cancel, with apologies. Then tackle things you can finish, one at a time if at all possible. Work mindfully at it, and enjoy the satisfaction that comes with getting it done. Procrastination can be a terrible stressor—we're always aware of what we *should* be doing while we're *not* doing it, and it's a real joy-killer and energy-sapper. Do a piece of it and check that sucker off!

8. **When Scheduling, Give Yourself Room To Breathe**
    If you find yourself scheduling yourself with back to back meetings, consider the possibility that you're an adrenaline junkie, running from appointment to appointment to feed your addiction. Leave time between things, to catch your breath, reflect on what's next, acquaint yourself with a calmer class of neurohormones that return you to equilibrium. Once you get out of the habit of racing, you won't be so eager to go back to it, I promise.

9. **Throw Something Out Every Day**

   Useless clutter is another low level, subliminal stress-producer. And we all know how quickly a clean surface can attract overwhelming piles of stuff. If you commit to throwing out one or two things a day, it really helps. And if you're one of those people who need to see your papers spread around you as you work (I am), just contain the surface area you allot to this!

10. **Keep Asking Yourself If You'd Rather be Happy or Right**

    A lot of stress is generated—for ourselves and others—by our need to be right, show we're right, prove we're right. And really, so what if we establish we're right? We cleanse our psychic pallet and de-gunk our day by letting go of an issue and moving on. Mind you, this is not the same as being a chump. It's about taking care of ourselves, and therein lies right relationship, clear focus, and yes, happiness.

11. **Don't Be Proud—Get Support When the Chips are Down**

    Sometimes talking things out with someone you trust will allow you to safely acknowledge your feelings, let off some steam, get you away from circular thinking and rearrange your mislaid perspective. Sometimes friends even have helpful advice to give. Sometimes they actually stop us from doing something really dumb.

12. **Practice Staying in the Moment**

    By mindfully going about your day, putting your awareness into what you are doing at the moment, you will be using even mundane, everyday activities as the focus of meditation, and simple as it sounds, you will regain peace and balance. Yes, peeling potatoes can be a route to spiritual attainment and inner peace!

13. **Notice Little Moments of Beauty and Sweetness**

    This sounds hokey but it works. Notice beauty around you and take a moment to breathe it in . . . same with a smile, a gracious act, a loving gesture. Practicing gratitude for these lovely bits and pieces of daily life is a potent way to de-stress, and it's contagious, too.

Evening Prayer for Peace

As the war in Iraq was heating up, someone suggested including this in The God Box:

In WWII there was an advisor to Churchill who organized a group of people who dropped what they were doing every day at a prescribed hour for one minute to collectively pray for the safety of England, its people and peace. There is now a group of people organizing the same thing here in America. If you would like to participate: every evening at 9:00 p.m. (EST), 8:00 p.m. (CST), 6:00 p.m. (PST), stop whatever you are doing and spend one minute praying for the safety of the United States, our troops, our citizens, and for peace in the world.

For Christmas that year, I sent out a prayer leaflet from Pax Christi USA to everyone on my Christmas card list. It includes a prayer for peace for each day of the week (they are included in chapter 13). From time to time, I closed the God Box with one of these prayers and encouraged participants to join the chorus of those praying for peace each night. To keep myself going with this practice, I posted a note on my computer and on my fridge. I also carry a copy in my wallet so I can pray for peace while I wait in lines or in traffic. To order a copy, go to *www.paxchristiusa.org*.

Elizabeth Gilbert in Her Own Words:
"Book One: Italy," from *Eat, Pray, Love*

When the question is raised, "What kind of God do you believe in?" my answer is easy: "I believe in a magnificent God."

—4—

Of course, I've had a lot of time to formulate my opinions about divinity since that night on the bathroom floor when I spoke to God directly for the first time. In the middle of that dark November crisis, though, I was not interested in forming my views on theology. I was interested only in saving my life. I had finally noticed that I seemed to have reached a state of hopeless and life-threatening despair, and it occurred to me that sometimes people in this state will approach God for help. I think I'd read that in a book somewhere.

What I said to God through my gasping sobs was something like this: "Hello, God, how are you? I'm Liz. It's nice to meet you."

That's right—I was speaking to the creator of the universe as though we'd just been introduced at a cocktail party. But we work with what we know in this life, and these are the words I always use at the beginning of relationship. In fact, it was all I could do to stop myself from saying, "I've always been a big fan of your work . . ."

"I'm sorry to bother you so late at night," I continued, "But I'm in serious trouble. And, I'm sorry I haven't ever spoken directly to you before, but I do hope I have always expressed ample gratitude for all the blessings that you've given me in my life."

This thought caused me to sob even harder. God waited me out. I pulled myself together enough to go on: "I am not an expert at praying, as you know. But can you please help me? I am in desperate need of help. I don't know what to do. I need an answer. Please tell me what to do. Please tell me what to do. Please tell me what to do . . ."

And so the prayer narrowed itself down to that simple entreaty—*Please tell me what to do*—repeated again and again. I don't know how many times I begged. I only know that I begged like someone who was pleading for her life. And the crying went on forever.

Until—quite abruptly—it stopped.

Quite abruptly, I found that I was not crying anymore. I'd stopped crying, in fact, in mid-sob. My misery had been completely vacuumed out of me. I lifted my forehead off the floor and sat up in surprise, wondering if I would see now some Great Being who had taken my weeping away. But nobody was there. I was just alone. But not really alone, either. I was surrounded by something I can only describe as a little pocket of silence—a silence so rare that I didn't' want to exhale, for fear of scaring it off. I was seamlessly still. I don't know when I'd ever felt such stillness.

Then I heard a voice. Please don't be alarmed—it was not an Old Testament Hollywood Charlton Heston voice, nor was it a voice telling me to build a baseball field in my backyard. It was merely my own voice, speaking from within my own self. But this was my voice as I had never heard it before. This was my voice, but perfectly wise, calm and compassionate. This was what my voice would sound like if I'd only ever experienced love and certainty in my life. How can I describe the warmth of affection in that voice, as it gave me the answer that would forever seal my faith in the divine?

The voice said: *Go back to bed, Liz.*

I exhaled.

It was so immediately clear that this was the only thing to do. I would not have accepted any other answer. I would not have trusted a great booming voice that said either: *"You must divorce your husband!"* or *"You must not divorce your husband!"* Because that's not true wisdom. True wisdom gives the only possible answer at any given moment, and that night, going back to bed was the only possible answer. *Go back to bed,* said this omniscient interior voice, because you don't need to know the final answer right now, at three o'clock in the morning on a Thursday in November. *Go back to bed,* because I love you. *Go back to bed,* because the only thing you need to do for now is get some rest and take good care of yourself until you do know the answer. *Go back to bed,* so that when the tempest comes, you'll be strong enough to deal with it. And the tempest is coming, dear one. Very soon. But not tonight. Therefore:

Go back to bed, Liz.[34]

Endnotes

1. Therese J. Borchard and Michael Leach, eds., *I Like Being Married* (New York: Doubleday, 2002), 19.

2. Belleruth Naparstek, *For People Undergoing Chemotherapy* (Cleveland: Image Paths, Inc., 1993).

3. Anne Lamott, "God's Inbox: Sometimes We Need a Little Help from Upper Management," *Salon* magazine, http://www.salonmagazine.com/dec96/lamott961202.html.

4. Ron Rolheiser, *Daybreaks: Daily Reflections for Lent and Easter Week* (Ligouri, Missouri: Ligouri Publications, 2005), 42.

5. Harold Kushner, *Who Needs God?* (New York: Fireside, 2002).

6. Lamott, http://www.salonmagazine.com/dec96/lamott961202.html.

7. The Virtual Community, www.rheingold.com/vc/book/1.html.

8. Rainie et al., *Strength of Internet Ties,* http://www.pewinternet.org.

9. Ibid., *Faith Online,* http://www.pewinternet.org.

10. Andrew Weil, MD, *Spontaneous Healing* (New York: Fawcett Columbine, 1995), 250

11. David Steindl-Rast, *Gratefulness, the Heart of Prayer* (Mahwah, New Jersey: Paulist Press, 1984), 105–106.

12. Ibid, 106.

13. Belleruth Naparstek, *For People Undergoing Chemotherapy.*

14. Steindl-Rast, *Gratefulness, the Heart of Prayer,* 134.

15. Ibid., 135.

16. Ibid., Back Cover.

17. Bernie Siegel, "Accept, Retreat, Surrender: How to Heal Yourself," *Share Guide: The Wholistic Health Magazine and Resource Directory,* www.shareguide.com.

18. Larry Dossey, *Prayer is Good Medicine* (New York: Harper San Francisco, 1996), 49.

19. Sharon Fish Mooney, "The Problem with Prayer Research," *Christian Research Institute,* http://ncf-jcn.org/facgrad/forum/DP804.pdf.

20. Dossey, *Prayer is Good Medicine,* 49.

21. Michael McCullough, "Prayer and Health: Conceptual Issues, Research Review and Research Agenda," *Journal of Psychology and Theology,* vol. 23, no.1, 1995.

22. William, J. Cromie, "Prayers Don't Help Heart Patients," *Harvard University Gazette,* http://www.hno.harvard.edu/gazette/2006/04.06.

23. C. S. Lewis, "The Effectiveness of Prayer," *Talking to God,* ed. John Gattuso (Milford, New Jersey: Stone Creek Publications, 2006), 79.

24. Dossey, *Prayer is Good Medicine,* 104.

25. *Milagros* (Spanish for "miracles") are used primarily in the Mexican and South American cultures as tangible representations of a prayer of petition or a prayer of

thanksgiving. Usually made out of silver, mixed metal, or tin, milagros are made in all shapes and sizes.

26. Elizabeth Gilbert, *Eat, Pray, Love* (New York: Penguin Books, 2006), 16.

27. Robert J. Wicks, *Everyday Simplicity* (Notre Dame: Soren Books, 2005), 127.

28. Joan Chitister, *Scarred by Struggle; Transformed by Hope,* (Grand Rapids, Michigan: Wm. B. Eerdmans Publishing Company, 2005), 2

29. Henri Nouwen, *With Open Hands* (Notre Dame, Indiana: Ave Maria Press, 1972), 73.

30. John Shea, *An Experience Named Spirit* (Chicago: Thomas More Association, 1983), 174–79.

31. Rabbi Krinsky, "Religion and the Internet," Dec. 8, 2000, episode no. 415, *Religion and Ethics Newsweekly,* www.pbs.org/religionandethics/week415/feature.html

32. *A tizzy is a "state of frenzied excitement or distraction, especially over some trivial matter" (Webster's New Unabridged Dictionary)* like preparing to leave for Philly!

33. Savannah's God Box decorates the cover of this book.

34. Gilbert, *Eat, Pray, Love,* 14–16.

Permissions

With a grateful heart, I acknowledge these authors and publishers for granting permission to share their inspiring words with you.

"I thank You God for most this amazing." Copyright 1950, © 1978, 1991 by the Trustees for the E. E. Cummings Trust. Copyright © 1979 by George James Firmage, from COMPLETE POEMS: 1904-1962 by E. E. Cummings, edited by George J. Firmage. Used by permission of Liveright Publishing Corporation.

"God's Inbox: Sometimes We Need a Little Help from Upper Management" by Anne Lamott, originally published in *Salon* Magazine (*www.salon.com*). Copyright © 1996 by Anne Lamott, reprinted with permission of The Wylie Agency LLC.

"Book One: Italy," from Eat, Pray, Love by Elizabeth Gilbert copyright © 2006 by Elizabeth Gilbert. Used by permission of Viking Penguin, a division of Penguin Group (USA) Inc.

Excerpts from *Everyday Simplicity* by Robert J. Wicks. © 2000 by Sorin Books, an imprint of Ave Maria Press Inc., P.O. Box 428, Notre Dame, Indiana, 46556. Used with permission of the publisher. *www.avemariapress.com*

Excerpts from *Seven Sacred Pauses* by Macrina Wiederkehr, © 2008. Used with the permission of the publisher, Sorin Books, an imprint of Ave Maria Press Inc., P.O. Box 428 , Notre Dame, Indiana 46556. *www.avemariapress.com*

Excerpts from *With Open Hands* by Henri Nouwen. Copyright © 1972, 1995 by Ave Maria Press, P.O. Box 428, Notre Dame, IN 46556, *www.avemariapress.com*. Used with permission of the publisher.

Excerpts from *May I Have This Dance?* by Joyce Rupp, OSM. Copyright ©1992, 2007 by Ave Maria Press, P.O. Box 428, Notre Dame, IN 46556, *www.avemariapress.com*. Used with permission of the publisher.

Excerpts from *Out of the Ordinary* by Joyce Rupp, OSM. Copyright © 2000 by Ave Maria Press, Inc. Used with permission of the publisher. Copies available at 1-800-282-1865 or at *www.avemariapress.com*.

Excerpts from *Prayers of the Domestic Church* by Edward Hays, © 1979. Used with the permission of the publisher, Forest of Peace, an imprint of Ave Maria Press, Inc, Notre Dame, IN 46556. *www.forestofpeace.com*

Excerpts from *Prayers for a Planetary Pilgrim* by Edward M. Hays, © 1989, 2008. Used with the permission of the publisher, Forest of Peace, an imprint of Ave Maria Press Inc., Notre Dame, IN 46556. *www.forestofpeace.com*

"A process for dealing with hardship" is adapted from *"Practicing Gratefulness in All Circumstances"* by Brother David Steindl-Rast and Patricia Campbell Carlson, *www.gratefulness.org*

Muslim, Jewish, Christian Prayer for Peace by Joan Chittister and *The Advent of the God of Peace: Reflections for Advent 2007* by John Dear are used with the permission of Pax Christi USA, 532 W. 8ᵗʰ St. Erie, PA 16502-1343, *www.paxchristiusa.org*

"Sharon's Christmas Prayer" from *The Hour of the Unexpected* by John Shea, published by ACTA Publications, 1977 (out of print) is used with permission of the author.

"Five Finger Prayer" is used with permission of the author, Paul Ciniraj, Kerala, India, *salemvoice@gmail.com*

"A Thought to Begin Your Day" reprinted from *Present Moment Wonderful Moment: Mindfulness Verses for Daily Living* (1990, 2007) by Thich Nhat Hanh with permission of Parallax Press, Berkeley, CA, *www.parallax.org*

"I Am There" by James Dillett Freeman is used with the permission of Unity, 1901 Blue Parkway, Unity Village, MO 64065-0001, *www.unity.org*

Excerpts from Daily Word are used with the permission of Unity, 1901 Blue Parkway, Unity Village, MO 64065-0001, *www.unity.org*

"Birth," "Death (for one who is dying)," "Death (for one who has died)" by Suzette Haden Elgin are from The Lovingkindness Survival Kit which can be found at www.forlovingkindness.org. © OCLS, 1998. Used with permission of the author.

"Magnificat" *(inclusive language)* by Fr. Stephen List and Fr. Michael Casey OSCO of Tarrawarra Abbey in Australia. Used with Fr. Casey's permission. Found at *www.liturgy.co.nz*

"A Prayer for the World" by Harold Kushner, © 2003 by Harold Kushner. First published by *Parade*. Reprinted by permission of Curtis Brown, Ltd.

"BR's 13 Lucky Tips for De-Stressing Your Holiday" by Belleruth Naparstek, published by Health Journeys, November 23, 2007, *www.healthjourneys.com* and For People Undergoing Chemotherapy, by Belleruth Naparstek, published by Image Paths, Inc. Used with permission of Health Journeys.

Lent: Sunday Readings by Megan McKenna is published by Veritas, 7/8 Lr Abbey St., Dublin 1, Ireland, © 2008, p. 197, *www.veritas.ie.* Used with permission from the author and Veritas.

Excerpts from *Psalms for Praying: An Invitation to Wholeness* by Nan C. Merrill, © 1996, 2000. Reprinted with the permission of the publisher, The Continuum International Publishing Group.

Excerpts from *Guerrillas of Grace* by Ted Loder, copyright © 1984 Innisfree Press. Used by permission of Augsburg Fortress Publishers.

Excerpts from *The Haunt of Grace* by Ted Loder, copyright © 2002 Innisfree Press. Used by permission of Augsburg Fortress Publishers.

"The Love of God" by Magdolene Myogosi, used with the author's permission.

"And So We Pray", following Alice Walker's quote from *Anything Can Be Saved* is adapted by Alexis Navarro and is used with her permission.

"The Hope of Loving," "Love Does That," and "Capax Universi," are from the Penguin anthology, Love Poems from God, copyright 2002, Daniel Ladinsky and used with his permission.

From *When Things Fall Apart*, by Pema Chödrön, ©1997 by Pema Chödrön. Reprinted by arrangement with Shambhala Publications, Inc., Boston, MA. www.shambhala.com.

"What I Learned from My Mother" from *Sleeping Preacher*, by Julia Kasdorf, © 1992. Reprinted by permission of the University of Pittsburgh Press.

Stations XII, XIII, and XIV: Joan Chittister, OSB, *Way of the Cross: Gateway to Resurrection*, p. 28-33, Benetvision, (www.benetvision.org). Used with Permission.

"The Lord's Prayer" (A Paraphrase) from *From Many, One* by Edward Francis Gabriele © 1995, Ave Maria Press. Used with permission of the author.

Scripture texts in this work are taken from the *New American Bible with Revised New Testament and Revised Psalms* © 1991, 1986, 1970 Confraternity of Christian Doctrine, Washington, D.C. and are used by permission of the copyright owner. All Rights Reserved.

Website information has been used with permission from each site:
www.gratefulness.org www.beliefnet.com
www.spiritualityandpractice.com
www.prayingeachday.org
www.sacredspace.ie
www.unityonline.org
www.worldprayers.org
www.mertoninstitute.org
www.healthjourneys.com

Obtaining permission for each of the prayers, poems, and reflections in this book has been a complicated and challenging process. For some (under 250 words) "fair use" was assumed. A few are believed to be in the public domain. If a required acknowledgment has been omitted, it is unintentional. Please notify the author or the publisher to rectify the omission in future editions.

Index

CPSIA information can be obtained
at www.ICGtesting.com
Printed in the USA
FSHW021519040619
58723FS

9 781441 553898